# The Heart of English

Nine to Fourteen

GW00507391

John Pearce

Oxford University Press   1985

**Acknowledgements**

Cover illustration by Sue Heap

*The publishers would like to thank the following for permission to reprint copyright material:*
Charles Causley: 'Cowboy Song' from *Collected Poems* (Macmillan). Reprinted by permission of David Higham Associates Ltd. Kevin Myhill: 'They Dared Him' from *Riverline*, the magazine of Wisbech Grammar School, Wisbech, Cambs. Theodore Roethke: 'Child on Top of a Greenhouse'. Reprinted by permission of Faber and Faber Ltd. from *The Collected Poems of Theodore Roethke*.

ISBN 0 19 919068 2
© John Pearce 1985

Oxford University Press, Walton Street, Oxford OX2 6DP

Oxford London New York
Toronto Melbourne Auckland
Kuala Lumpur Singapore Hong Kong Tokyo
Delhi Bombay Calcutta Madras Karachi
Nairobi Dar es Salaam Cape Town

and associated companies in
Beirut Berlin Ibadan Mexico City Nicosia

*Oxford* is a trade mark of Oxford University Press

Phototypeset by Tradespools Ltd, Frome, Somerset
Printed in Great Britain by Spottiswoode Ballantyne Ltd., Colchester

# Contents

## Introduction

This book is a manual intended for teachers who find themselves teaching English without claiming a specialist competence in the subject. It thus seeks to help two main kinds of teacher. The large majority of those working in junior and middle schools, or training to do so, have main subjects other than English, but their general professional competence provides some solutions to the problems of English. The other kind is the growing body of teachers, mostly in secondary schools where falling rolls have left a choice between adapting and leaving the profession. Many such teachers are given a class or two of English.

The audience I have identified is also engaged in teaching within a well defined age range: English does not begin to acquire the status of a distinct subject much before the third year of the junior school or the first year of the 9-13 middle school. On the evidence of the DES Secondary Survey, non-specialist English teachers in secondary work tend to be concentrated on years 1 and 2, with some work in year 3. These facts have defined my target area as the ages from 9–14. Because I am seeking to cater for junior, middle and secondary teachers I have sought to be not too precise about levels and ages and school structures, and hope that you, the reader, will allow a suitable flexibility in interpreting such references as I make.

I have tried to be realistic about the schools where my readers are likely to be working. Most schools provide some choice of textbooks and teaching resources, but the choice will be more limited than the almost complete freedom about how these are to be used. There will be a head of department or language leader to approach for advice, but that person may not actually be used to giving it. Most schools will have a reasonable library of fiction but enabling the children to get at it may call for tact as well as tactics. Most schools can impose quite harsh conditions on teachers without realizing it – I have seen the quiet-voiced probationer fighting to read poetry against the thunder of the music department next door, and the young teacher trying to inculcate French vowels in a fully tiled cookery room that reverberated like a cathedral – but such problems can be resolved, if the need for something better is explained.

The views expressed in this book do not reflect the policies of the authority where I am employed or the opinions of its teachers. It is true that such clarity and coherence as the book can claim will have emerged from years of conversation with those teachers, in classrooms and staffrooms and especially on courses where they have done me the welcome courtesy of dissenting. Many will find traces of themselves in these pages. I hope they will feel acknowledged in being recognizable, if only to themselves.

I once knew a Rabbi who had escaped the Holocaust and worked for Jewish-Christian relationships. Invited to address a congregation of funda-mentalist Christians in America he began thus: 'The Good Lord gave us ten commandments – but cannot have meant us to keep more than five at a time. After all,' he would add, visibly counting with his fingers, 'you can only count that far, because you need the other hand to count with.' However many commandments, advices or suggestions you read here, remember that Rabbi.

John Pearce *Huntingdon, January 1984*

Chapter 1

# Reading for understanding

Between the ages of 9 and 14 immense changes take place in how children read. The majority of them achieve a dramatic increase in their speed of reading, the range of material they tackle, their grasp of detail, and in their ability to bring together strands of meaning from different parts of a book. The starting point of the three chapters in this part is that these great changes should not be taken for granted: the teacher has a responsibility to steer them because a policy of letting them happen allows them not to happen at all in some pupils. The teaching programme needs to recognize changes as they take place, organize the reading progress of pupils so as to foster them, and take account of long-term as well as short-term needs in developing approaches and responses to books.

The first chapter in this part of the book sets out the aims of the work and draws the immediate conclusions, particularly as they bear on comprehension work. The second chapter outlines a set of specific strategies for developing the intermediate reading skills. The third offers a series of basic patterns on which the reading programme can be organized.

Reading and writing skills matter more than ever. We sometimes hear futuristic suggestions that we are 'moving beyond print'. Well, one or two boffins might be, but ordinary people will depend on print for the lifetime of children now in school, and their dependence will be greater, not smaller. A visit to any Job Centre will reveal that for a majority of jobs you now have to write a letter or fill in a form, whereas 30 years ago most merely went for an interview. The VDU screens on the modern computer are harder to read than ordinary print. Literacy remains the open sesame to our rights, our full membership of society, often to employment, the best use of savings, and all sorts of other things. Moreover the literacy that matters tends not to be the basic sort any more: the intermediate reading skills of knowing where to search for information, how to extract it, how to interpret it and apply it are increasingly important. The same holds for being able to write coherently. I have chosen in this book to deal with the age range from 9–14, which leaves only two years before the legal school-leaving age. All young people within a very short time now will face additional training if they are not in further education or still at school, and that fact testifies to the need for more developed skills. If the basis has not been laid in the 9–14 stage, the additional work of later stages will be much harder to do.

## Aims and what they cover

Learning to read is rightly viewed as the first priority for all children. All teachers recognize that the process continues after the age of 9. The learning that happens if this continuation is haphazard is significantly smaller than if the reading progress is properly planned. Such planning needs to start from some aims. I am going to focus on the averagely competent 9 year old, who can read a book at the top end of most reading schemes or a straightforward children's novel. We would want him to have or develop these qualities:

**1** An alertness to detail, so that he distinguishes word from word, sentence from sentence, singular from plural, past from present etc.
**2** Responsive interest in what he reads, the quality of not being a mental blank taking it all in without comment or reaction.
**3** A disposition to pick up the many meanings in what he reads, to infer, read between the lines, spot what is implied as well as what is said.
**4** The skills of making the fullest use of the meaning–clues in a text.
**5** Above all, the motivation and self-confidence to become a fluent reader of various kinds of text.

We shall come back to most of these aims, but the most important of the questions and findings in research about reading have been in the area of the nature of fluent reading. The lessons of the soundest research do not support some very common practice, mainly because that practice rests on too simple a conception of what 'reading' really is. Many would say it is to 'decode print', but that is a cover term embracing very complicated processes including eye-movements (very irregular ones at that), immensely rapid judgements about text scanned, text just read, text coming next, how they fit together. Such a phrase as 'make sense of print' denotes a process where the print is seen as a given, fixed, to be 'made sense of', whereas the reader in reality brings a complex body of knowledge to bear on it that makes it much less fixed, capable of steadily greater understanding. This dynamic view of reading is now very firmly established, and with children of age 9 it is essential to move on from infant school methods of 'hearing children read'.

## Hearing children read

The main research on this topic was done by a Schools Council project at Liverpool in the 1970s called *Extending Beginning Reading*. Its book of that same title showed that teachers who heard all their pupils read were able to give them an average of 30 *seconds* a week. It is far better to come to terms with this, set out to hear fewer of them for very much longer, and work with each child on the weaknesses shown up. The researchers found a direct link between success in reading between 7 and 9 and being allowed to read at length, silently and without interruption, with occasional discussion of the books they have been reading. The most successful classes were those with the *least* emphasis on 'hearing children read'. If this is true of children between 7 and 9, it is even more true of older ones, and the advice that arises bears on them too:

1 Curtail drastically the attempt to hear many children read briefly from books selected by the teacher.

2 Time spent with individuals needs to be much longer, while happening less often.

3 Provide periods in which every child is reading a book of his own choice, without interruption or chatter, increasing the length of these periods steadily.

4 Set out to create more teacher time for individual work by making the children self-reliant in finding spellings.

5 Above all, develop group work in which groups can run themselves so that the teacher can work with a group uninterrupted.

For older age-groups it is only necessary to add two suggestions: the silent reading should usually occupy a whole period where English is given six or seven timetabled periods (as it usually is), and the self-reliance about spelling needs to be extended in some degree to marking, a point elaborated in my final chapter.

## Plan for reading

The reading curriculum will not develop the skills mentioned in our list of aims if the development is not planned to have that effect. A great deal is now known about the way in which the reading skills of a competent 11 year old differ from those of an average 9 year old, and about how children can be helped to acquire the additional skills that make that big difference. I shall set some of it out in more detail in the next chapter.

The reading curriculum is best planned if it takes advantage of the nature of language rather than runs counter to it. In particular, speech is learned before writing, and spoken language has a long history, in any language, prior to the evolution of writing. So the reading strategies will try to exploit the children's normally expert proficiency as talkers in order to foster their skills as readers. By the same token, however, handling print is a learned skill, not a natural one; as such, its learning will be more successfully achieved if the process is made as pleasurable as possible.

So while we can order the components of the reading curriculum in many different ways, to suit the needs of particular classes or buildings or fit the contents of particular stock cupboards, an efficient reading programme will be planned, will foster diverse skills in diverse ways, will be related to natural speech as well as to writing, and above all will seek to motivate children to become fluent and effective readers.

## Individualize reading

The core of the programme must be the books provided in the classroom. In a 9 year old class several children will be nearing the end of a conventional reading scheme or branching out into the supplementary and extension readers associated with it. This branching out should be achieved with as many children of that age as possible. Where the school uses a structured reading and language programme that goes beyond a reading age of 12 or 13, the abler pupils should not be allowed to rest on their success with it: wider choice of their own personal reading from a library needs to become the spine of their work. Every pupil aged 9 or 10 should be learning how to select novels for personal reading from a school or classroom library. The book stock used for the purpose needs to have been given a broad grading or colour-coding so that children know where to start looking and do not waste time on inappropriate choices. Organizing that coding is a job for the language specialist on the staff rather than a novice or a non-specialist.

The process of choice itself is not as simple as it may look, and needs some participation from the teacher. Children of 9 or 10 can be dismayed by the spectacle of a whole shelf of library books, let alone a whole library, and the teacher's role in helping them is treated in more detail in Chapter 3. Any programme seeking to individualize the children's reading will make quicker headway if the majority of the books are paperbacks, but books which are tatty or dog-eared or without a legible spine are inviting the children to treat books badly. That is why front-cover display of children's fiction is important, grading will help, and a close watch on the reading histories of the children will identify the pupils who need direct help.

Some children can read but won't; others would read if they could, but can't. The reluctant reader, that is to say, is different from the slow reader. The reluctant reader is usually male and his reluctance usually relates to fiction: do not be surprised by the scale and complexity of the hobby-reading that such a child will often undertake. Equally, however, do not let that enthusiasm become his sole reading diet. Reluctant readers will sometimes have to be compelled, but a good reading programme will include tasks that engage them. Prediction work such as 'How does this story finish?' and inquiry tasks such as 'You ought not to have been surprised by that ending: why not?' can go a long way to overcome reluctance, and the range of such tasks is described in the next chapter. Older boys may cling to a belief that fiction is 'sissy' when they clearly know better, but the strategy of tolerating the choice of frankly sadistic novels like *Skinhead* is an admission of defeat. To knuckle under to the teenage boy's reluctance to read fiction of any sort will convey to him that you do not think it important either, and it is precisely by the teacher's response to such challenges that real values become known and real respect is established.

The slower reader used to be caught between reading matter that was too difficult and books where the content or the level of interest was too childish. A number of the larger publishers now offer series where the level of interest is firmly above that of the primary school child while the level of reading difficulty is held down to stipulated levels. (One of the better series is the Longman *Knockouts*, some of which tell very mature stories with rare clarity.) There are now quite enough books of this kind to make it possible to treat slower readers on the same basis as ordinary ones: there is no justification whatever, nowadays, for putting the slower readers at the back of the room with a worksheet or other undemanding task while the rest of the class gets on with its personal reading. The reading-extension work described in the next chapter will allow the same policy, although some special materials or tasks may be necessary within the overall framework. The real business of intermediate reading is, if anything, more important to the slower reader, not less.

## Reading for information

So far I have written about the reading curriculum as if it were entirely composed of fiction, but that has been for convenience. Informational reading raises very similar issues, with two main differences. Except where reading difficulty is very severe, children will pursue information sources with extraordinary drive if the motivation is strong enough, and will read material far in advance of their nominal reading ability. The other difference from fictional reading is that children are not born with the skills of knowing how a library is organized or how to trace a particular piece of information in the books in which it may be hidden. These 'survey skills'and 'study skills', as they have come to be known, have to be taught, and schools have increasingly recognized the need. Where the curriculum is in separate subjects the task usually falls to English departments, but the need arises much earlier, especially in the context of topic work.

Here again, the publishing houses have recognized a widely-felt need and have produced a variety of materials to help schools to meet it. The most valuable single set of materials is at present that issued by Oliver & Boyd and developed by John Cooper under the title *Directions*. The series starts with a short book suitable for young juniors and runs all the way to material for lower secondary pupils. The books lend themselves to a range of age levels and do not try to monopolize that English curriculum. Unusually, the later additions to the series (*More Directions*) are just as good as the early books and their definition of study skills is a broad one.

One of the objectives in developing book-using skills is of course to help children learn to synthesize information from several sources. Copying it out is a stage in that learning process, and teachers have to show some determination in persuading children to grow out of it. Making plain your determination to stop verbatim copying will go a long way, while penalizing those who persist will bring the message home – e.g. 'Now re-write this in half the length without opening the reference books'. It is even better to forestall verbatim copying by setting up topic work in groups of two or three so that the group has to synthesize its individual findings before starting its final writing work.

## Comprehension and understanding

In English teaching 'comprehension' has acquired a special meaning, one a shade different from its dictionary meaning. So the title of this section is not quite the paradox it may seem.

Let us look at a practical example. It is one of those secondary departments where children are encouraged to talk because it 'fosters their oral skills'. The children are 12 year olds, sitting in desks arranged in ranks of pairs. After some discussion of a homework, the course books come out and the page and exercise numbers are written on the board. Margins are ruled, dates inserted, and the first answers written down. The quicker ones are already into discussion. The text they are answering questions about is an extract from somebody's memoirs of the death of the Old West with the disappearance of the American buffalo. Couple No. 1 are in fact discussing last night's cup match on the TV; couple No. 2 are mutually contemptuous of glacé kid for fashion boots; couple No. 3 have done eight of the ten questions and are deep into fishing floats for pike; and so on. When all have completed the 'work', transferring the required bits of information from book to exercise book while pursuing their far more engrossing conversations, it will all be piled up for the teacher. She, in turn, will have to get 3 DY tomorrow to do another like it so she can have time to mark this lot . . . .

Now let us take another example: a classroom of top juniors, orderly and quiet. The group work is well-grooved. Each group switches from Maths (Alpha and Beta) to English (Once a Week Comprehension) to Topic (Castles) to SRA. The SRA work is additional to the English. The teacher is busy hearing her three backward readers read. The group working on SRA collects its cards, takes them back in silence, completes its answers, records it all, and so to the next task. In the English part of the cycle the group read 188 words of text; in the SRA part, 244 words. In the same amount of time required for these two parts, the class next door has been engaged in silent individual reading and has read an average of 1,800 words . . . . The next week, alerted by an in-service course, the teacher experiments: she takes four of the SRA cards, covers up the passages, and asks the children to see if they can still answer the questions. Average score: nine out of ten.

All this labour is impressive. The work leads to huge numbers of ticks and very few crosses. The children feel very secure in a routine they know. But what do they feel about it? What do they learn from it? I watched a class 'do a comprehension' on a very informative passage about the decline of the cotton trade. Next day I went back and set them ten one-word-answer questions seeking basic facts they had read in that passage. Average score: one out of ten. We discussed why, and one boy, aged 13, put it neatly:

> 'Well, we only do them passages to answer the questions.
> We don't have to read 'em to *understand* 'em . . . .'

Another one was overtly cynical:

> 'S'long as the answers look like a sentence you get a mark: last year
> I used to write some answers deliberately wrong, to see, an' if they
> were in sentences I always got a tick.'

The class obviously endorsed these attitudes, and many specialist English teachers take them for granted.

At this point let us look again at our aims, set out at the start of this chapter. They refer to *responsive interest, a disposition to infer and read between the lines, skills of making the fullest use of clues to meaning.* The conception of reading with and for understanding built into these aims is a very active one. The logic of these aims points to ways of using written text that differ quite sharply from conventional comprehension activity. Most comprehension work, whether in text books or on work cards, rests on the assumption that its purpose is to increase the pupil's vocabulary. Everything we know about language development suggests that vocabulary is not the main problem: using the evidence and meanings on the page will reveal most of the vocabulary meanings. The problem is to bring children to use the evidence in front of them. That requires the building up of habits, attitudes and skills, and most conventional comprehension work leads to neutral or negative attitudes, positively bad habits, and omission of the important skills. What alternatives will do better?

## Some examples

COWBOY SONG

I come from Salem County
Where the silver melons grow,
Where the wheat is sweet as an angel's feet
And the zithering zephyrs blow.
I walk the blue bone-orchard
In the apple-blossom snow,
Where the teasy bees take their honeyed ease
And the marmalade moon hangs low.

My Maw sleeps prone on the prairie
In a boulder eiderdown,
Where the pickled stars in their little jam-jars
Hang in a hoop to town.
I haven't seen Paw since a Sunday
In eighteen seventy-three
When he packed his snap in a bitty mess-trap
And said he'd be home by tea.

Fled is my fancy sister
All weeping like the willow,
And dead is the brother I loved like no other
Who once did share my pillow.
I fly the florid water
Where run the seven geese round,
O the townsfolk talk to see me walk
Six inches off the ground.

Across the map of midnight
I trawl the turning sky,
In my green glass the salt fleets pass
The moon her fire-float by.
The girls go gay in the valley
When the boys come down from the farm,
Don't run, my joy, from a poor cowboy,
I won't do you no harm.

The bread of my twentieth birthday
I buttered with the sun,
Though I sharpen my eyes with lovers' lies
I'll never see twenty-one.
Light is my shirt with lilies,
And lined with lead my hood,
On my face as I pass is a plate of brass,
And my suit is made of wood.

*Charles Causley*

This poem was one of three offered in duplicated form to a group of half a dozen 12 year olds in a far from exceptional school where 'bright' children were rare. There were no questions posed, orally or in writing, but the children clearly knew what to do. They spent a few moments deciding which of the three poems to read, and fell for the attractions of the title of this one. For fully two minutes they read it, in silence. Then, looking round the group for a second, one of the boys began very quietly humming the tune of *The Big Rock Candy Mountain*. The smiles of recognition over, a girl said, 'I don't get it. What's it got to do with that song anyway? Where's the point?' An extract from its beginning hints at the discussion that went on for more than ten minutes:

| | |
|---|---|
| *Tricia*: | I don't understand this last verse. |
| *Gail*: | Nor do I. |
| *Tony*: | You know what Mr Warner said: pin it down to a word. |
| *Tricia*: | The last two lines: why's he got a brass face? |
| *Eric*: | It isn't only his face, is it? |
| *Gail*: | What do you mean? |
| *Eric*: | He's got a suit that's made of wood. I think that must mean he's in a coffin. |
| *Several*: | Eh? Nonsense! What rot! |
| *Tony*: | Wait a bit, you lot. His Maw sleeps alone on the prairie . . . . . *she*'s dead. His Paw's gone away. His brother's dead. Why shouldn't this one be dead too? |
| *Gail*: | Coz he's lookin' back an' rememberin' 'is family. |
| *Tricia*: | I agree with Tony. Why else does he say 'I won't do you no harm'? I think it's a ghost story. |

A deal of dispute followed between Tricia and Tony on the one side and the other three: even Eric, who saw the point of the last stanza, could not grasp the idea that the whole poem might be a ghost story device, and kept looking for the place in the poem where the cowboy dies. The others came round to Tony and Tricia's view bit by bit, and when the teacher arrived they described their view of the poem. He asked them if they could put a tune to it. Yes, they could. 'Why then,' he asked, 'does such a strange poem have such a cheerful tune?' The children worked out for themselves that there was meant to be what they called an argument going on between the words of the poem and the feeling of the tune.

Perhaps it is labouring the obvious to suggest comparing that kind of process with asking the class to sit down and look at a poem in silence and then write sentence-form answers to such questions as 'What does *zithering* mean?' Less obviously, if your approach is like that it restricts the kind of poems and prose you can ask the children to deal with. Written 'comprehension' questions virtually drive out of the English classroom texts which are subtle, complex, not immediately obvious. That such texts have a place and are perfectly manageable by children who have been led to pose their own questions is a commonplace of enlightened English teaching.

My other example is from a class of boys and girls aged nearly 14 – right at the end of the summer term of their third year in a small rural comprehensive. The teacher had taken them through a long discussion of some local anti-nuclear agitation and had been puzzled to find a majority of them with minds quite closed to the idea that the protesters might be perfectly sane and serious people. He said 'Usual sixes' and distributed copies of this poem:


THEY DARED HIM


Tommy has dropped his Atom Bomb
Upon the nursery floor
Until the dust has cleared away
His little brothers cannot play
Toy soldiers any more.

Teddy's hair is falling out
From Gamma radiation
Jane will have a busy hols,
Six defenceless little dolls
Need decontamination.

You should have seen the mushroom cloud
Rise upwards to the ceiling.
Nanny says they can avoid
Having all the cows destroyed
As some of them are healing.

Tommy has dropped his Atom Bomb
Upon the nursery floor.
He has completely spoilt the fun,
It takes an ordinary gun
To make a decent war.

*Kevin Myhill*

The reading was silent, and there was a surprisingly long period in which, in their groups of six, none of the children would say anything. One boy turned round and said:

'Sir, who's Tommy and Jane?'

The question was referred to his group and the silence broke abruptly. One group thought it was simply funny. Two groups, independently, came to the view that it was a comment on the Falklands campaign and other small-scale wars. A fourth group spent most of its time trying to see how the first two lines could make any kind of sense. The fifth included twin brothers who recognized the string of allusions in *nursery, toy soldiers, Teddy, hols, Nanny, spoilt the fun*:

'I think he's getting at something.'
'You mean rich people?'
'Not quite: it's not their money he's after, it's their habits...'
'You mean employing a nanny and having a nursery and all that......?'
''Sright. Stuck up people with stuck up kids.'
'An' these seem to have come distinctly *unstuck*, eh?'
*Pause*
New voice: 'But it's the parents he's getting at, not the kids.'
*Pause*
'The parents in that sort of class?'
'The class as runs the country. That's it: it's a political dig, a..,
a... what's the words, like that piece Sir read us about telling lies over Vietnam...'
'Oh, satire.'
'That's right...'

No transcription can convey the unmistakable note of glee in discovery as the speaker refers to *Tell me Lies about Vietnam*, which the teacher had read them during a sequence about pop music and its lyrics.

Equally, no written comprehension questions can bring about that central sequence of perceiving the nature of satire first and finding the technical label for it afterwards. Nor can they generate the social skills that allow and tolerate silence or the linguistic skills that play the ideas back and forth like a tennis ball with such economy.

The difference in quality and depth between answering written comprehension questions and this kind of discussion has to be taken a little bit on trust until the teacher has come to experience it for herself. At its best, comprehension by discussion is a process of working out what a writer is 'getting at' by a series of stages of insight. Those stages cannot be programmed: they depend on the perceptions the pupils bring with them. Hence, the business of selecting and wording and placing particular questions (or of choosing not to do so) has to be a teacher's personal task, not one to be delegated to textbook or work-card. Real comprehension, that is to say, needs to be done orally. On the scale of longer works such as a novel or a play the same principle applies, with due allowance for differences of scale and genre.

## An example using a novel

Let me illustrate the way in which skilful handling of a novel can move far beyond the limited scope of the written comprehension question without facing the children with literary analysis beyond their powers. A middle school's top year group, aged 13–13½, was organized for English into three ability sets. The 'top' set, rightly described by the teacher as a top set in maturity as much as in ability, had read Ann Holm's *I Am David*. This now well-known novel traces the escape of a boy of 12 from a prison or refugee camp in the Balkans, through a series of adventures (all of them quite credible in themselves and free of melodramatics) on his way through Europe. In each of these episodes he encounters an aspect of the adult world and grows up accordingly. He contrives at the end to present himself on his mother's doorstep in Denmark. Within the assumptions of its opening situation, the novel is compellingly written, but those assumptions demand a rather too ready suspension of disbelief. We do not hear how David and his mother came to be separated, how the boy came to be so far from her, how he knew so precisely where to go while she could not find him, and so on.

The teacher, whose own subject was history and who had never taught English before, had read the novel with the class and found himself more and more discontented with the loose ends. Ultimately he felt the plot too contrived and the treatment sentimental, and he had read enough novels on his own account to feel some confidence in his judgement, but he was unsure of his pupils' reactions.

He began by soliciting opinions:

> 'Obviously, you enjoyed *I Am David*, yes?'
> A chorus of assent: 14 girls and 10 boys clearly approved.
> 'What particular things did you like, then?'
> A series of answers denoting a class well used to discussing books:
> 'The bit when David...', 'The man he met in...', 'The whole Italy stretch was very vivid, just like Italy is really...', 'The ending made me cry for days...' and much else.
> 'Did anyone dislike it?'
> *Silence*

'Very well then, I would like you to work in your usual fours and spend 12 minutes making notes for Topic A which I'll put on the board. Then we'll go on to Topic B which I'll put up later. Group chairmen-for-the-day to make the notes and we'll review both sets together.'

Topic A read as follows:

Suppose you are to write a review of *I Am David* for the school magazine, and that you want to give it a very favourable one. You need to identify at least three but not more than five substantial reasons in support.

The work went well and the notes came in. The teacher observed that there were 18 minutes left. He turned to the blackboard, replaced A with B and changed 'favourable' to 'unfavourable'.

The groups looked puzzled and the discussion was very desultory for a while, but they warmed to the work and the notes that came in on Topic B were strikingly more solid than those on Topic A: the reasons were stronger and there were many more of them with much less in common between the groups.

In the next English period, two days later, the teacher issued a sheet that summarized the notes on Topic A: all six groups had found two main reasons, four groups had found two more, for viewing *I Am David* as a good book. The pupils protested: they had not thought things out properly at that time, they had changed their minds, and so on. The teacher refused to be put off: 'But these were your views, honestly held when you noted them down. And the reasons are sound enough, aren't they?' The pupils reacted by citing some of their material from Topic B, but the teacher held them to admitting that there was truth in their answers to *both* topics. In the discussion it was possible to watch children learning for the first time that no book is all good or all bad, than any book is a mixture of strengths and weaknesses. After a look at a similar sheet setting out the group views on the book's weaknesses, there was discussion of the balance between them, and there followed a homework task: 'In your own opinion, do the good qualities in *I Am David* outweigh the weaknesses, or the other way round?'

It would miss the point of this example to object that the book in question is really one for 11 year olds (with whom it is often used, but I return to that issue in a later chapter). What the teacher did here was to break down some very complex issues of judgement and balance into manageable blocks, and to do it in a way which exactly matched the state of maturity and readiness of the class. He also brought them to manage those blocks in such a way as to provide an oral rehearsal of many of the ideas and uses of language they would want when they came to write their individual pieces. The careful balancing of group discussion with a written output, whole class exchanges with the teacher, and individual writing gives the work a shape and brings to the reading a completion that are uncommon, and at the same time compels a significant movement forward in the children's powers of judgement. It is a process that needs repeating, certainly not with every novel or play, but often enough to equip young people with the rudiments of critical judgement before they come to a GCE course in literature and before they are cast entirely on their own resources in deciding what or whether to read for their own adult enjoyment. For that is the end of the development which has to start with learning how to read a whole book and understand it as more than a set of separate chapter-length stories. The comprehension curriculum, if I may call it so, has an importance that exposes most comprehension exercises as trivial.

Chapter 2

# Teaching skilful reading

The four activities described in this chapter are quite well-known: prediction, cloze, sequencing and questioning. After looking at some objections, the chapter suggests some further practices for more detailed work.

## Prediction

No efficient reader takes a text word by word and adds each one in turn to his stock of knowledge. Not only do efficient readers move their eyes in jerks and leaps; not only do they take a surprisingly large part of a text 'as read'; they do these things because the bit of text they have read enables them to form a pretty good idea of what is coming. 'Reading' thus becomes a process of very rapid matching of actual to predicted, with re-matching only when the reader meets a slight surprise. This principle is worth using in the classroom because work which fosters the skills of prediction greatly increases the pupil's ability to handle new material. Predictive skills, that is to say, are an integral part of fluent reading.

The simplest form of prediction is to ask a class or a group to read a chunk of a story and guess or predict the next chunk. Each chunk can be thrown on an OHP screen, but the best format is to have the chunks on separate pieces of card or arranged one to a page in a booklet. Using a single sheet with one-inch spaces between each chunk is a short-cut which usually defeats the object of the exercise. Figure 1 (page 17) is an example, based loosely on a well-known short story by Somerset Maugham. The class or group has to decide, on the evidence of the first chunk, what they think happened next. The oral give-and-take of reaching this decision will include a persistent search in the text for clues and evidence, and groups not yet used to this will need the example of the teacher's questioning in starting them off on it. The group leader then unveils the second chunk, with similar predictions to be made on the next one, but this time on a different body of evidence. The cycle is repeated through the sequence, but at any point children can be asked to suppose that the story goes no further and to write their own version of the conclusion. (This is, in passing, a much better stimulus to story-writing than the well-known practice of simply giving children an opening sentence.) Group oral prediction can be organized in groups or pairs, and the reading level of the material can be adjusted if necessary, but children often read 'above themselves' in it.

One of the merits of doing prediction work as a separate exercise, quite apart from sharpening children's attention to the detail of what they read, is that it can afterwards be applied to anything else they happen to be reading. This is especially valuable where the writer is planting clues and foreshadow-ings that the readers seem to be missing, and the more literary the text the more

About the time of Queen Victoria's diamond jubilee, Albert Foreman was the caretaker of a school in a big city. One day a new Headmaster and a new Vicar discovered that he could not read and write. They thought this was a handicap in his work.

The Vicar and the Headmaster consulted the School Board and decided that Albert Foreman would have to go. Very sadly, they called him in to see them and gave him a month's notice.

On his way from that dreadful interview, Albert looked for a sweet shop: he wanted a packet of nuts or something to occupy his mind. He walked a very long way through the streets near the school but could not find a sweet shop.

Albert and his wife slowly got over the shock of his dismissal, but his search for a sweet shop gave him an idea. When his month's notice ended, he and his wife rented a shop with a flat above it, and before very long they had set up in business as a tobacconist and confectioner. He was careful always to stock a variety of nuts.

Three years later the Foremans had done well enough to open another shop, and during the next five years they were able to open three more. They put a manager into each shop they had started and went to live over each new one. Every shop was opened at a site where it was a long way from any other shop like it, and all of them did very well.

Every week Albert Foreman took his takings to the bank. One day, when he had been in business for twelve years, the manager asked to see him. He told Mr Foreman that he had a great deal of money in his account, and he ought to put it into a savings account or into stocks and shares so it would earn some interest. Albert did not like this idea at all, and said he would think about it.

A year later the bank manager tried again. Albert explained that he did not want to be bothered with all those papers. The manager said it could be done through the bank and all he had to do was sign the forms. Albert explained that he couldn't read or write, and would not be able to do that.

'Good heavens', said the bank manager. 'You have twelve thousand pounds in the bank and you cannot read or write! Where would you be if you had been able to?' Albert Foreman smiled. 'I can tell you that, sir: I would still be caretaker of St. Mark's Church of England Primary School...'

*Figure 1   Based on Somerset Maugham's short-story, 'The Verger'.*

this kind of detail will signify. An elementary example occurs in the verbal habits of the characters in *Wind in the Willows*, a more subtle one in the use of rhyme in the poems quoted in Chapter 1.

## Cloze

A more precise application of the same idea is known as 'cloze procedure'. This entails writing or printing out a text with some of the words omitted in such a way that the length of the blank space gives no clue to the word deleted. As a rule the omissions or deletions occur every tenth or seventh word, after a 'run in' of a few lines to establish a context. Thus, the task of the      is to work out what word      required in each case to fill      blank space, and to do so such a way as to fully      the sense of the passage.

There are many variations on this idea: one can delete only the nouns or the adjectives, or delete so frequently that the puzzle becomes almost insoluble.

The procedure relies on two facts: all language has built into it a deal of redundancy, so that even the sparest prose tends to say most things, if not twice in full, then more than just once; and prose has an intricate web of internal connections. Thus, if we fill the blanks left above and identify the evidence for doing so, we see the links being made:

| | |
|---|---|
| pupil/group | inference from earlier parts of this chapter |
| is | application of knowledge of verbs |
| the | application of knowledge of phrase structure; 'each' is possible but would repeat the word |
| in | application of knowledge of prepositional phrase structure |
| restore | inference from *fill* and *fully* |

This activity brings wider knowledge of language into play without requiring that knowledge to have technical labels, which is exactly what happens when we read a text that is a shade demanding. Some of the deletions are supplied, moreover, from clues which occur after rather than before the blank. Cloze compels pupils to look at text more closely than conventional comprehension questions, and the talk about meanings that it gives rise to is often fascinating. There is no need to insist that every answer be the author's exact word until the texts being used are of literary quality or technical in subject-matter.

## Sequencing

The story in Figure 2 (page 19) consists of six sentences, and they have been set out in jumbled order. The essential task of sequencing is to reassemble them in correct order. The mechanics of organizing the work in class can vary, of course, as can the level of the material, the ease or difficulty of rearranging it, and the way children are grouped for the activity. Ideally, a class of 9 year olds will work in groups of three or four, perhaps in pairs, and the school will have a bank of sequencing materials graded from the very simple to some which are hard enough to make adults disagree about the sequence. The point of the work lies, however, less in getting the order right than in the debate which attends each placement.

For example, the sentence 'To their surprise, they lost their money' is placed by many children as the last one in the sequence, and the notion that the sentence which draws the moral of the fable (i.e. 'However many times . . . would lose their money') is the proper conclusion of the sequence seems to pose difficulties. The debate has to focus on the relation between *lost* and *would lose* and what these tenses signify, although the children would not use the term 'tense' in such a context.

As with cloze procedure and prediction work, the focus of sequencing is on attention to text, particularly to the way text hangs together. The sequencing task cannot be performed without such attention: for example, we select the opening sentence by its lack of features which refer to previous sentences, such as *they* in the second and fourth sentences, and we arrange one sentence after another by reason of the same kind of feature. Thus, *the player with the ivory*

One visitor brought out his set of crudely carved, unpainted pieces and set them before his host's set of finely carved and valuable ivory.

To their surprise, they lost their money.

In ancient China, it is said, travellers of a certain class were expected to show good manners to their hosts by playing chess with them.

However many times they backed the player with the ivory pieces, nine times out of ten they would lose their money.

By the custom of the country, each player was required to use his own set of chessmen.

The onlookers laid their usual bets on the result, and most of them backed the player with the ivory pieces.

*Figure 2   Chinese chess – an exercise in sequencing.*

*pieces* in the sentence given last must come after the sentence given first, and that in turn comes after that printed third because *one visitor* refers back to *travellers*. The ability to make such connections and links between the parts of a text is critically important in almost all branches of education beyond age 14 and is decisive for work in higher education, but no better way has been found to help children acquire it. By comparison with the laboured explanations of this paragraph, echoed in comprehension questions, group sequencing is economical, very simple to do, and effective.

What is not simple, of course, is the preparation of the material. Here are some of the ground-rules:

1   Choose stories which are self-contained and complete, preferably with a pithy point at the end. It is easiest to start with episodes from books the children know.

2   Some grammatical points are worth avoiding (by recasting the text a bit): sentences more than 20 words long, sentences that begin with because-, when-, if- or although- clauses, and stories where *he* or *she* can refer to two characters of the same sex.

3   A story for sequencing should have not less than five nor more than ten segments, but each segment can be (and after a while should be) more than one sentence. The prose needs to be as natural as possible: reading scheme text is not a good source.

4   Sequencing cannot be done successfully with the segments arranged out of order on a single sheet: that is a short cut that penalizes the less able. It matters that children can move the segments about on the table to try out different arrangements. If the room is not to drown in a sea of slips of paper, the material needs to be mounted on card or laminated, and a set can be held together with a treasury tag.

5   Sequencing material needs to be clearly printed or typed.

Initially, of course, teachers will draw on story books and novels for sequencing material, adapting it freely. As the pupils become more skilled, it is possible to increase the level of difficulty quite severely, and mixed-ability classes aged 12 and 13 have responded remarkably to the challenge of writing material for sequencing work with pupils a couple of years behind them. Pupils practised in doing this can be challenged to devise material where the 'right' sequence remains genuinely a matter of debate even for adults.

## A note on method

Mention was made earlier in this chapter of the need for the teacher to do some active 'setting up' of prediction work. The same holds for cloze and for sequencing. Merely putting the material in front of a group and stating the task is not enough: the children may carry out the task but they will miss most of the benefit, because that lies in the discussion of possibilities, the interchange of ideas about words and meanings, the constant matching of perception to evidence. How that proceeds in a group will depend on how the group has been led into its possibilities, which only the teacher can do. And because the work is small-group activity there is not really any shorter route for the teacher than sitting down with each group in turn and doing the activities with it.

Even then, the teacher's role remains critical: the skilled teacher will set a group to, say, a prediction activity and let them get on with it for some time, but she will be alert to the way the group's body language reveals frustration and will call back for what may be the crucial stages of the work. Again and again in these activities a brief question or comment from the teacher will set going a new perception and fresh argument, and insight and evidence are the high road to our aims.

## Questions

The fourth route towards our target of fluent, responsive reading which is also perceptive about inner as well as outer meanings is much the easiest to set up: it asks pupils to look at pieces of text and decide for themselves what the important questions are that should be asked. Pose-your-own-questions is a method to be seen in action in both the examples on pages 9–11. The brief given to the children is to write down between three and five questions about the piece to which they would like answers. At first, of course, the questions they write will be the sort they are used to seeing in comprehension books and work cards, but the teacher can steer them into questions about what comes out between the lines and later on about what lies beyond the piece altogether. What do you do with the questions?

1 Arrange the class in pairs of pairs so that each pair can have another pair answer the questions.

2 Take soundings out loud about the commonest questions and set two of these for groups of six to discuss.

3 Give one pair of pupils the task (usually much welcomed in lieu of something more conventional) of analyzing the whole set for homework, using the commonest ones for class discussion later.

The pupils may jib at writing their own questions, sometimes because it can be hard to find texts which exactly match their level of skill and their state of readiness. There is a handful of questions the teacher can use instead, many of them now in the tomb-like sterility of textbooks: is this a good title, what title would you give this, what evidence is there here about the age/sex/nationality/beliefs of the writer, what would you have put into this that the writer left out, and so on. There is a simple way of varying this, by putting on the blackboard a string of five or more statements, some of them bland but some seemingly outrageous, and asking the groups to arrange them in order of appropriateness or truth about the text.

## Some attractive blind alleys

There have been many commercial attempts to 'update' work in English, especially in recent years when research into reading has become an industry. The vogue for multiple choice questions is an example, and it has waned as teachers have learned from experience how difficult it is to write them properly. It is worth noting three other practices which are often cited as up-to-date and 'backed by research', and seeing where they relate to what is being said here. Reading 'laboratories', whether from the publisher best known for them or from a number of imitators, are fundamentally the conventional comprehension textbook dressed up in work-card format and wrapped in a largely spurious precision of grading. The research work published in 1979 seemed to show that SRA laboratories achieved marked results, and so they did in the conditions of the experiment, which was intensive, short, in lieu of all other work of the same kind, and tested with the sort of written sentence-answer tests we are trying to get away from. The experiment was bound to be circular, because it accepted the definition of comprehension embedded in the 'laboratory'.

The same problem arises with attempts to be 'scientific' about teaching comprehension by reducing it to its 'component skills'. The research evidence is overwhelming that comprehension is not an entity built up of 'sub-skills'. The best we can do here is to take on board one of the most useful distinctions developed in the field, that made by Barrett, between literal, inferential and evaluative comprehension. These lead to 'checking questions', 'filling in questions' and 'opinion questions', and give us, not a guide to notional stages or skills in children's learning, but a criterion for judging the quality of a comprehension activity. If all the questions are literal, you may be sure the children can answer most of them with the kind of inattentive boredom illuminated earlier. If they are in some cases inferential, the reader is at least likely to refer to the text again to see what he missed. If he is asked to be evaluative, to reach some sort of judgement, he has to think. Taking Kevin Myhill's poem quoted on page 11, part of its charm is that there are few literal questions worth asking. An inferential one would be:

What are the cows suffering from?

and an evaluative one might be

Has the writer achieved the rhythm accurately in every line, and if so what does that suggest about the quality of the writing?

The literal–inferential–evaluative framework is also useful in designing sequences of material, and has been used successfully in some published examples. (The *Scope for Reading* series published by Holmes McDougall is a case in point.) But that use does not justify the idea that comprehension can be taught by marching solemnly through one sub-skill after another up the hill to the top. Lunzer and Gardner put it plainly:

> We conclude that individual differences in reading comprehension should not be thought of in terms of a multiplicity of specialized aptitudes .... such differences reflect only one general aptitude: this being the pupil's ability and willingness to reflect on whatever he is reading.
>
> *The Effective Use of Reading* (p.64)

The other way in which conventional and unsuccessful practice can reassert its influence in English work owes a great deal to the practice of initial training institutions, where 'discussion' is held to be a Good Thing, and Teacher Talking is held to be a Bad Thing. There are several objections to whole-class discussion with children between 9 and 12. In practice, whatever the theory may say, only a handful of the pupils get a look in: the majority would avoid anything so public and exposing as speaking in the hearing of a whole class. Consequently there tend to be silences, which the teacher is usually trained to fill in rather than leave unfilled, so that what purports to be a discussion can often be a case of teacher talking for most of the time. Again, much of the teacher's input to such lessons can take the form not of provocative statements leading to dissent, but of questions which provoke the game known to some pupils as GWITH – or Guess What's In Teacher's Head.

## Some objections

All very well, you will say, but my pupils misread texts all over the place, employers complain that apprentices misread their manuals, and what we need is real standards in comprehension. Surely we have to help build their vocabulary?

Well, perhaps, but the pupil who has reached our target will ask some questions about your use of the term 'build': if vocabulary consists of bricks, walls are more than bricks and buildings more than walls. Are teachers really in the business of lexical bricklaying? The metaphor is misleading. There are better ways of attacking the problem, but before turning to them we ought to note that if someone misreads a text the fault just might lie with the text. Perera has assembled a striking set of examples, from books published for children to use, which positively invite misreadings, with a set of categories that the blunders fall into.

Such blunders bring us to the first line of attack. A text is duplicated and distributed to the class or group. The first task is always to sift it for individual words the children are not sure about. The group makes a list, each member in turn looks one up in the dictionary, while another writes down the meaning. Then the group get out their red and blue pencils and start underlining – the parts of the text they can understand in blue, the parts they cannot understand in red. Pairs or threes can work through their own red patches, or the red patches can be analyzed like the questions referred to above. (In secondary schools the best material is continuous prose from textbooks in other subjects being used by the class.)

The next line of attack is to ask groups to swap-read the passage. This device requires one of the group to read the text aloud in such a way that when he comes to a vocabulary word (noun, verb, adjective, adverb) he makes a fractional pause and other members of the group in turn provide a swap-word or synonym. When groups of children are used to the technique the reader can be asked to pause less often, or only on words beginning with a vowel, or only on words he thinks will be particularly awkward. Words which no-one in the group can swap for have to be written down and looked up. (Incidentally the work gives precious practice in reading aloud.)

A third device is known in some classrooms as TPS, which is short for Talking for the Partially Sighted. It arose from a regular exchange between a large junior school and a neighbouring special school, where the special school children who spent a day every term in the junior school included a group of partially sighted girls. The teacher noticed that her pupils were eager to read their own writing to these girls, but that some of the words were beyond them, so that the readers had to substitute words and phrases to simplify the language as they went along. She replicated the situation later, having some of her own pupils play the role of the visitors, and asking others to take information-books and do the same simplifying-as-you-go process in reading aloud to them: the listeners would signal a not-understood item with a raised finger, and the teacher noticed that slow-learners who took part in this showed a striking diminution in the frequency of the finger-raising after a few days. It would be nice to be able to report what happened when the teacher asked her class to play 'fingers' on her own talking and reading to them, but history records it not.

One other device for bringing children into closer attention to words and detail in written material is 'writing down'. Teachers who work with sixth form and fifth form students know that they can very often show remarkable skill with the very young. Left to develop the relationships in their own way they can make admirable infant helpers. The same notion seems to operate when older secondary pupils are asked to take some of their own school material (such as the notion of continental plates, or how a vacuum is made) and rewrite it so that children of 10 or 11 can understand it. Some middle schools have used this device, asking the top class to re-tell a story for the first year, but it is not as easy as it looks at first glance. The reason is that 'writing down', in real life, has to be totally lucid if it is to succeed, and that imposes a focus on the language and wording rather than on the content. Even so, the attempt and some discussion of it would be more useful work on written material than the same amount of time spent answering simpleton comprehension questions.

## Comprehension once a week?

Well, yes and no: more often than that, and less often. Children need to be seeking meanings all the time, and sometimes to be set to seeking them, but formally 'doing a comprehension' almost never. We have seen how the weekly-exercise routine imposes an insidious diminution of the quality of the reading material. Because it is usually done by whole classes, the material has to be selected for the lower-middle range of the children. Because it is usually treated as a written exercise (and for very respectable reasons) the texts have to be the sort that permit literal questions with simply written answers. That makes comprehension needlessly dull for children and teacher alike when it ought to be exciting. The fact that GCE and other examination papers use formal comprehension questioning with candidates aged 16 does not make that a good model for much younger pupils – in most educational fields the effect would be the opposite.

None of this means that we have to do without a core textbook unless we want to: it is not course books we need be afraid of, but the inert acceptance of unwisely selected ones. It may be helpful to list the criteria to be used in selecting textbooks designed to provide children with a wide variety of reading material that meets the need for some of their reading to be systematically purposive:
1   The passages need to be of solid length rather than snippets. The simplest yardstick is that children have a much stronger sense of doing 'real' reading if they turn the page. The device of text printed over artwork is viewed by most children as suitable only for infants.
2   We are among other things teaching children to learn study skills such as chasing references and noting their sources. Course books ought to set a good example and give the author and source of each extract, which should be a real author and a real book.
3   Questions printed at the end are in reality unhelpful, for reasons already given in this chapter.
4   The balance between reading for meaning and other textbook-based activities ought to be nearer five to one than two to one – the reasons for this are given in Chapter 9.

The question must arise in many junior schools how a course book chosen on the basis of these criteria would relate to a carefully made spine of basic and extension readers. Provided the activities that children are asked to pursue in connection with those readers are real ones, rather than formalistic or time-occupying chores, this approach would amount to the same thing. Similarly, a much more broadly based and thorough-going scheme like Ginn's *Reading 360* (no doubt the first of many of its kind) offers pupil activities of many kinds organically related to the books in the scheme. It is a pity, though, that so few of its users have adopted the full width of the pupil activity work and have tried instead to press on through the levels: used with the supplementary materials, Level 10 of *Reading 360* is quite demanding for children aged 10, and so for other levels.

At the secondary level the steady reliance on a course book to provide at least one of the weekly English lessons is much less common than it used to be: English departments seem to opt more for an open regime in which teachers draw sets of books from the stock according to what they want to use, rather than a uniform one where each year uses the appropriate volume of a course book. The difficulty with the former pattern is that it entails much careful planning and even then can have problems when two teachers want the same materials, but most teachers find it a rewarding approach. The difficulty with the latter is that course books written for five years of the secondary school are almost bound to be much better for some ages than others. The non-specialist teacher working in a department that offers choice will find my suggested criteria useful, but even that help cannot take away the burden that faces any teacher of English selecting work for her classes: even if the extracts to be used are all in a thoroughly safe and well-tried course book, she has to read them in advance and make decisions about what to select and how to approach it. It is in the planning and preparation stage that a well written teacher's book can make a great difference, and while my strong liking for John Seely's *Oxford Secondary English* is becoming widely shared, it is the quality of its Teacher's Books that makes this series valuable to all kinds of teachers.

# Chapter 3

# The reading curriculum

Most children at the age of 9 are working through a reading scheme. By the age of 14, young people need to be able to range as widely in reading as their studies or hobbies may take them and as deeply in literature as their interests may lead. This is a massive transformation, and we would misunderstand it if we saw the change between 9 and 14 as mainly one of new levels of skill. Certainly there are particular skills to learn and we have already looked at some of them, but they will be little use without the framework which gives them point and use. That framework is the theme of this chapter. Like other chapters, it will try to digest in a helpful way a field known to specialists on a much more detailed scale, but its material may well be less immediately recognizable. After dealing with a handful of the issues that occupy the concerns of specialists, I shall outline the principal classroom approaches available.

## Aims and issues

Let me return to the aims we began with. One of them was the aim of enabling children to develop the motivation and self-confidence to be fluent readers of various kinds of text. 'Various kinds' points to history books and hobby manuals and science textbooks and newspapers as well as stories and teen magazines. Mastery of such a range may be the aim for school leavers, but the means to that end for most between 9 and 14 will be story books – fictional prose narrative, with poems and plays and short stories as variations. Most material within the reading capacity of children of these ages, moreover, will be of book length (i.e. novels as distinct from short stories). The motivation and self-confidence have to relate therefore to whole books, have to survive intense competition from the school curriculum and the attractions of other media and interests, and have to endure while the demands of other roles in life displace spontaneous reading for long periods. A reading skill survives only if it has become a habit, and a reading habit will survive only if it is well grounded by the age of 14. Our task, then, is to organize the reading of novels in such a way as to elicit enthusiasm in our pupils and to build up in their thinking an assumption that novel-reading is worth while in itself. By comparison with reading schemes and composition and spelling and the other things in this book, that is for many teachers something of a novelty. If you are one of those teachers who have not yet discovered children's literature, you have a treat in store.

Mention of a reading skill and a reading habit involves making a generalization: most reading habits are peculiar to the individuals who own them. They are the products of highly individual processes of learning, experience, and attitude-formation. Some of us feel not quite complete without a book 'on the go', but teachers for whom fiction is a pointless activity need to suspend their prejudices about it. This is because for most children the reading of fiction is a pleasurable route to some important skills – being able to find one's way round a library's shelves, scan a shelf of titles, scan a blurb and a page of contents, skim a few pages of text to size up a book's pertinence or use. Less obvious book-using skills are the ability to reject a book as disappointing after a few chapters, to use an index with accuracy, and identify what sources to explore in searching for information. These skills can be acquired only by children familiar with books, which means children who have enjoyed books, which means (between 9 and 14) mainly novels.

Beyond the logic of our stated aims, of course, there are more potent reasons still. Why should we teach literature at all? Stripped of all pretension there are three answers. Schools are not provided merely to churn out economic mechanisms: literature is as rewarding to the competent reader as music or painting or freshwater fishing to those with the competence needed for those fields. Secondly, it is not the purpose of schools to churn out mere audiences for horoscopes and agony columns: literature exists on a huge scale which embraces instruction and exaltation about every significant aspect of the human condition and we betray our pupils if we do not give them access to it. Thirdly, human beings must order their universe if they are to survive, an ordering that has to apply on the global scale, the personal scale and every scale in between – and literature offers feeling and insight that bear on that ordering from the most utopian optimism to the narrowest selfishness, which we ignore at our peril.

These aims and their consequences lead us at once into some central issues about what children read in school. If literature is to be so vital, how should children move from reading schemes to novels? Answer: by blurring the distinction between them and encouraging children to take responsibility for their own reading choices. When should this happen? As soon as is reasonably practical: the urge to put all the children's reading into a formal scheme is too tidy-minded for most children's good. If the best readers are those who met complete books before learning to read (in such picture stories as Carle's *The Very Hungry Caterpillar*), they will also be the first to want to read 'real' books and should be encouraged. What is the right balance between the teacher's decisions and the pupil's choices about what he reads? The teacher governs the choice by selecting the stock, and within that structuring the pupil's choices become a learning process. These issues are in some cases large and theoretical, but others become very practical and even technical. There is not space to cover all of them, but three of them need to be tackled squarely.

## What happened to the classics?

A quick view of a typical primary or middle school stockroom will not reveal many class sets of 'good books'. The teacher in her 30s or older who expects to find a set of some favourite 'classic' is likely to be disappointed, and it is worth explaining why. 'Classic' is a status word, and each generation has its own set of classics. Until the 1950s, the literature available for children tended to consist of a crude choice between classics and rubbish – between Ballantyne and Bulldog Drummond, R. L. Stevenson and Biggles, Brontë and Blyton. Many children, consequently, were given classics to read before they were ready for them, so that the very term 'classic' has often had an uneasy mix of regard and rejection in its meaning. In the last 30 years a growing body, which by 1970 had become a flood, of well-written children's fiction has filled the gap between rubbish and classics, much of it so good that the notion of 'classic' status has lost all meaning.

The process by which particular books become invested among adults with the status formerly ascribed to *Treasure Island* and the *Just So Stories* can still be seen. A children's novel of considerable length receives an admiring critical press, and skilful marketing exploits the good start. Within a few years the book acquires a large body of admiring adult readers, whether the book has enduring appeal for children or not, and such a kinship between book and readers bespeaks genuine literary power. We can see this process, and the implied literary quality, in the standing of *Watership Down* and *Lord of the Rings*, which only a minority of children would read through on their own. Classic status has thus become largely a commercial matter, and it is necessary to move beyond such considerations if our judgements of books are to be sound. The relevant literature is mentioned below.

## Reading level and reading age

Books do not have reading ages. It is not particularly helpful to think of children as having reading ages either, but reading age has become a convenient simplification for describing how well children do on a reading test. (That no short and simple reading test is accurate enough to justify labelling a child with a reading age is quietly forgotten. At best a given reading age usually means 'somewhere between four and six months either side of the figure given'.) Publishers have sometimes coded their children's fiction with a suggestion about the age for which it is suitable, and such indications should be heeded, not because the texts have been scored for reading age or level but because most editors know their job and know their readers. Even so, I have seen many instances where a class reader has gripped the interest of a very wide range of reading ability in a class, and children tend to be better judges of what is too hard and too easy than do teachers.

There has been much energy put into the question of readability in the last two decades, and a straightforward book on the subject by Colin Harrison, *Readability in the Classroom*, covers the ground well. There are over a dozen 'readability formulae' which seek to assign varying weightings and scores to particular attributes of text, and on that basis make it possible to give each text a readability level or rating. All these formulae are arithmetical. They depend on counting words and syllables. The number of words per sentence will always be part of a formula. So will the number of syllables per word. So text like this that uses many short sentences will score as very readable. But if it uses continuous multiplicities of exceptionally polysyllabic formulations (like this), its score will go up. It is a fascinating study, and for specialists can be useful in sharpening their awareness of some of the sources of reading difficulty. But Harrison is quite definite that a reader whose motivation is strong enough will overcome quite formidable linguistic obstacles in his reading. Teachers can watch this readily: quite slow readers who want information badly enough will wade through impossibly difficult reading to pursue their chosen hobbies like machine knitting or making model aircraft or CB radio. The problem for the teacher is how to generate such motivation in a whole class.

In any case the features of prose text that readability scoring can measure are not the whole story. If I write a sentence that starts with an if-clause, and if I follow it with a second if-clause, I am putting two obstacles between the reader and what the sentence is about. Sentences that come straight to the point and put the qualifications afterwards will help the reader. Even more, sentences will help the reader if they come straight to the point and put the qualifications afterwards. This kind of sentence-order problem cannot be measured but strongly affects response. For example, most children find the Roman Britain novels of Geoffrey Trease much easier reading than those of Rosemary Sutcliff for this reason. But there is no way of applying this insight to a system of grading books for their possible readers. If a book's appeal can be to children over a two-year range, and a child's ability can be anywhere within a twelve-month span of reading age, the best we can hope for is some helpful approximations. Against that background, children have to learn how to make choices.

## Fiction, fantasy and 'realism'

Adult literary criticism is full of debate about the novel and its relation to documentary narrative, about the stance of the persona of the narrator, and searching experiment in form. Some of the same diversity holds in children's fiction too. Most novels are written in the tradition of the omniscient but anonymous narrator, or that of the participant character writing in the first person, and the latter has given rise to a telling variety in which the narrator is a child. Such stories as Betsy Byars' *The Eighteenth Emergency* and Gene Kemp's *The Turbulent Term of Tyke Tiler* arouse sharply differing reactions among adults: some see the one as funny and perceptive and the other as unbearably coy and self-regarding, while others reach the opposite view, but the discussion is best conducted with the children. More seriously, is a book about a child on his own in Victorian London, living in a garret and terrorized by its slum gangs of children, to be seen as a historical novel or, as almost all its young readers will see it, as a fantasy? Where and how do young readers begin to grasp that some elements in a story they are reading are 'real', and what does 'reality' mean in such a discussion? These and the many related issues to arise from professional discussion of children's literature have given birth to a handful of very useful books that deal with the more theoretical questions. One of the earliest first appeared in Canada: *Only Connect* (1969) includes some outstanding papers that have not dated. *The Cool Web* (1977) is also a collection of short papers, but edited and organized with impressive clarity and beautifully designed and printed. There is a set of a dozen accounts by authors and the critical papers include some about classroom responses (notably by Aidan Warlow) which command great respect. Among a number of more historical and academic books about children's literature, John Rowe Townsend has written books which bear the stamp of a successful novelist, but Fred Inglis' *The Promise of Happiness* contains a wide-ranging and incisive set of judgements which stem from a consistent outlook and provoke valuable re-thinking.

Most recent and perhaps most helpful of all is a set of course booklets from the Open University published for its free-standing in-service course for teachers P530, *Children, Language and Literature*. The main book offers a sequence of activities and readings, supplemented by an audio cassette and background notes, with a densely packed booklet listing resources, information and sources of guidance on selecting children's literature. The practicality and scope of this material are beyond praise: it refuses to hold the teacher's hand, refrains (as I shall) from identifying 'ten best buys', and has useful suggestions in almost every possible circumstance. The material is in the same broad tradition as *The Cool Web*, and is deservedly gaining influence through numerous study-groups of teachers.

A typical class of 12 year olds choosing books from a good school library will take books ranging all the way from innocuous tales like 'The Famous Five' to futuristic SF; from sentimental romance to social-realist stories about life in the contemporary raw. As we have noted, the way children respond to these varieties of fiction does not match the adult notions of realism, history, fantasy and so on. (For example, does the Biggles yarn of the original period, in the 1930s when Biggles flew biplanes, strike a child born in 1973 as history or fantasy, and in either case does it matter?) We are only slowly coming to understand how fiction affects those who read it, adults or children. The seminal thinking behind most modern work was done by a professor of psychology: the key paper published by D. W. Harding in 1962 is given in *The Cool Web*. It rests on a passage worth repeating:

> . . . To obliterate the effects on a man of the occasions on which he was only an onlooker would be to profoundly change his out-look and values.
>
> Besides looking on at events in progress we can be spectators in memory or imagination of things past and things anticipated; further, we can release our imaginings from practical limitations and consider what might have been and what might be if the restrictions of reality were suspended. Even in looking on at actual happenings the spectator often grossly distorts what occurs, misleading himself by a variety of unconscious mechanisms; in memory and anticipation the unwitting distortion of fact and probability is even greater; and in fantasy even the intention to

control thought by the measure of possibility is largely
relinquished. In all the forms of fantasy, whether dreams,
daydreams, private meanings or make-believe play, we give
expression to perfectly real preoccupations, fears and desires,
however bizarre or impossible the imagined events embodying
them.

For anyone unsure about the potential of fiction for releasing and shaping the
imagination of young minds, Harding's paper is essential reading. The old
notions of identifying with a character or 'living' the experience of a novel's
events alongside its characters become the simplistic and naive responses they
are: 'The basic process connecting the onlooker with any event, real or
fictional, involving living things, is that of imagining.'

Most serious thinking about children's literature since the mid 60s has been
built on this foundation. Without wanting to trivialize a complex debate, we
can extract three general points:

1   The diverse reading histories of a given class of children will do far
more than determine their measured reading attainment. Thence derives
their readiness to choose, their susceptibility to being engaged by an
author's opening page, their knowledge of how and whether to become
onlookers at imagined events. This diversity will resist the urge to
control it, and will respond best if we seek to guide and steer it.

2   A pupil reads a book and develops a relationship with it. A class will
likewise develop a relationship with a book. The two relationships are
not of the same kind and it is a mistake to think that skilful teaching can
make them so. They complement each other and are equally necessary,
but separate.

3   Children have a less experienced sense than adults do about what
constitutes reality, and thus a more fluid definition of it. So they have
wider notions of what is imaginable, permissible within acceptable limits
of imagination, and it is important not to be too literal-minded with their
imaginings. Imagination and reality will have to come to terms with each
other soon enough.

## Classroom approaches 1

The conventional approach in many schools a generation ago was the 'class
reader', and it survives. Traditionally each pupil is provided with a copy and
pupils take it in turns to read aloud. The teacher may suddenly nominate a new
reader (sometimes seeking alertness in the class rather than any other objective)
or she may interpose with a question about meaning. Where the pupils can
handle aloud reading of the chosen text without preparation it is perhaps an
acceptable approach, and in the grammar schools of the past it tended to be the
only approach to a novel. In the mixed-ability classes that predominate in
junior, middle and lower-secondary contexts today it is open to some

objections. Most readers lack the reading skills to do full justice to a text in that setting; the presence of a critical audience increases their anxiety and they read the worse for it; the teacher's interventions break up the flow. More seriously, only very rarely do the individual pupils read for long enough to ease into reading aloud as such. Worst of all, every pupil is in reality reading the book at his own pace, usually ahead of the oral reading but in some cases trying desperately to catch up.

There are strategies that will minimize some of these weaknesses. One is for the teacher to read every other passage herself, which does wonders for the pace and reduces the numbers ahead on their own because they recognize that a skilled reading is worth following. Better still is for the teacher to organize some preparation: each pupil who is to read is assigned a passage of substance to get the reading ready in advance. The effect of this on the quality of reading, not as performance but as an act of translating writing to speaking, can be remarkable. More systematically one can use the principle of producing a class play and give every pupil something to do in the exercise which is integral to the success of the whole. At the simplest level a book will sometimes allow each pupil to be given a chapter to prepare – Nicholas Fisk's fast and sparely written *Snatched* is an instance, and many other novels can be parcelled out in three and four-page blocks to individuals. One of the reasons for taking a novel as a class reader, however, is that the procedure brings in books that few of the class would (or in some cases could) read for personal reading. This holds for Dickens and Hardy and a large number of novelists with pupils of 13 and 14, as well as for some children's novels with younger pupils. It is just this kind of text that most suffers from conventional reading-round-the-class, and a modest amount of planning and forethought will pay great dividends. My example is a well-known children's novel, but the technique will apply to many others (I have used it myself with Thackeray in a sixth-form and have seen it done brilliantly by top infants).

O'Brien's *Mrs Frisby and the Rats of NIMH* looks at first glance like a nursery fable. In reality it is a demanding read for 10 year olds. The rats, whom we do not meet for over 60 pages, have been caught for laboratory research at the otherwise unexplained NIMH establishment of the title. The experiments have made them intelligent, literate, capable of social organization and of no mean technical ability. They escape and develop a complex and technically advanced society, and in the course of escaping and developing their lives afterwards they have experiences which are described in detail. For example, they learn how to manipulate the fastenings of their cages and have some problems at the top of the air-conditioning shaft which is their escape route, and the spatial imagination in the reader that is called for by the writing is unusual. The author makes few concessions to his readers, but the story is inventive, funny, full of ironical digs at human society and not without its excitements. While the novel is an excellent choice for a teacher to read *to* a class of 9 year olds, it would be even better to read it *with* a class of 10 year olds.

This involves some planning. First, identify the big dramatic set-pieces which can be parcelled out to a group of children for preparation. Let the group appoint its own producer, give the producer a few notes about how to go about the job, and set the group a stringent time-limit for its rehearsals. *Mrs Frisby* has between four and eight such scenes. Second, identify as many two-man and three-man scenes as possible, which will vary in scale from three pages to an eight-page chapter, and assign for each scene a pupil for each part and one for the role of narrator. The incentive of being personally involved will overcome the children's initial uncertainties about how their piece fits into the story and in any case it is wise to have the list of assignments prepared but to give them out only a day or two before each is needed. The list is likely to leave only a handful of children, some of whom can be rehearsed in straightforward aloud readings of narrative, some of whom can be given explanation jobs – for example, to find out about air-conditioning ducts and make some drawings to explain O'Brien's text, or to make a working model of how the rats moved the concrete block where the Frisby family lived. The object is not to enable the class to 'do' the book without having any of it read aloud by teacher or pupil, but to engage every pupil in the book in a direct way. The approach takes more time than a 'straight' read, but classes that are accustomed to it can even refuse the role of being read to, so keen on these alternative approaches do they become. The dramatized parts invite and often receive background music, sound effects, and other attributes of radio drama.

There will usually remain parts of a book that have to be read aloud without benefit of dramatic methods, and the skill of being able to read aloud in the hearing of the class is too important to leave until the secondary stage. Even this, therefore, repays a little planning. The teacher should sit down with the text, work out where the changes of reader should fall, identify passages suited to the skills of less able readers, and try to predict the questions that need asking. If the teacher knows where the breaks are coming she can avoid interrupting a reader's flow by holding these questions until the break occurs. The class quite unused to reading aloud needs to have its individual passages identified so the pupils can prepare the reading, and each passage can then have some substance: a five-line snippet is not worth while, and most 11 year olds should be able to make half a page of a novel quite audible with decent expressiveness after a few minutes to prepare it.

Some novels do not lend themselves to follow-up, any more than do many poems. It is not necessary to feel compelled to wring a book dry in search of useful writing tasks if the experience of reading it has been valuable in itself. Where questions and writing tasks are used, they should be judged mainly by whether they make the children go back to the book with new kinds of attention. Asking them to re-tell the story puts children at a hurdle which fells many adults, and it is unhelpful to ask them to speculate about causes or effects the author has not told us about. Where a novel implies a comment on the real world it is fair to ask about the implication, as in the incident in *Mrs Frisby* where the rats decide to emigrate, leaving the technology behind, and a group of them disagree, break away on their own, and are electrocuted. Some of the useful questions to ask about a novel occur as it goes along and many of these can be found in the techniques suggested in the previous chapter.

## Classroom approaches 2

The commonest alternative to reading round the class is group reading. The class is divided into groups, usually on a basis of ability, between four and seven strong, and each group is provided with the necessary copies of a book suited to its abilities. Putting the slower readers together will not demoralize them of itself: children are well aware of the span of reading level in a class, which may be as wide as seven years of reading age. What will demoralize them is leaving them to their own devices. While each group can simply be left to read its book taking it in turns, the group work is more useful if it is directed by some kind of study programme related to the book they are reading, a 'Book Study'. (The Book Study can also be used with individual reading choices, of course.) Such cards should avoid comprehension questions, for reasons we have explored. The first task should be a discussion one, making the group try out ideas they would not develop on their own, and each Book Study should include scope for a personal reaction, the reader's likes and dislikes. Other questions to adapt to each book include 'Should you have been surprised by . . . (an event in the story, the ending, etc) . . . and if not, why not?', 'What events struck you as not very credible but worth keeping in, and why were they worth keeping?', 'What parts of the story would you have liked to see rewritten, and in what way?'. The best tasks for writing in a Book Study context call for some group discussion first, which give the teacher the job of deciding when the talking has to stop.

Book Study work does not all have to be a follow-up. For example, one can ask pupils to write about being kidnapped children of wealthy parents, and then have them compare the work of professionals like Nicholas Fisk and K. M. Peyton; or to write about being evacuated from London at the age of eight in 1939, without father or mother, to be billeted on a widower of 62 in a small country village, and compare the results with Michelle Magorian's gem of a novel *Goodnight Mister Tom*.

## Classroom approaches 3

Even with some of its better variations, reading round the class is passive for most children. Group reading is usually better in this respect, but out on the opposite extreme is individualized reading. This is both the logical upward extension of the use of reading schemes and the natural procedure with a mixed-ability class. It calls for an adequate library, some basic rules for the children, and nerve on the part of the teacher. Most children will read a novel they have chosen from the library in three weeks, allowing for some stimulating of the laggards, and for a majority of children not more than half the stock provided for their age-group will match their reading level. This is why such an approach needs many books: at least 300 novels in a class library, and in a school library catering for a 12-class middle school at least 3,000 fiction and as many non-fiction would be desirable, although the system can be worked on something over half those levels. Using a school rather than a class library basis makes it necessary to instruct the pupils in how to use a library.

The ground rules probably need to include some listing of books on a basis of 'all pupils should read one of these'. Unless there is a class reader in use as well, it does greatly help to have some common points of reference and areas of knowledge to bring to bear in discussing books. Children need deadlines, dates by which they will be expected to be ready to change their book, and insisting on changes even when books are unfinished will cut the losses as well as stir the children who would like to have finished. Above all, the process of exchanging the books needs care and active help. How might it work?

Let us imagine a class of 26 children aged 11, half-way through first year at a comprehensive school, gathered for their exchange period in the library. Eight of the children are on established 'lines', intending to read another book by a known author or a sequel or part of a cycle (Arthur Ransome, C. S. Forester and many more have written them). Seven more have a good idea of what they want: a book of a film, a teacher's suggestion, a friend's recommendation. There are 11 others, and the teacher has about 30 minutes in which to match read to need. Two boys want war stories. 'Which war?' 'Oh, one with sailing ships.' 'Have you tried Hornblower? The name's a laugh but the stories are good.' A girl has adored *The Secret Garden* but F. H. Burnett's other book is a bore. She is offered a handful including two by Philippa Pearce, and Janet Hitchman's *King of the Barbareens*: one can't tell if it was the ethos or the orphan situation that drew her. An able boy has read his fill of the Narnia books but welcomes something similar 'but not wishy washy, you know . . .'. The teacher points him to Ursula Le Guin's *The Wizard of Earthsea* and says 'Give that ten minutes and come back if you don't like it.' Two girls, socially mature for their age, hooked on Enid Blyton, confess to being bored with the 'Famous Five'. Again, is it the social context, the element of 'adventure' or the skirting round the difficult issues – who can tell? The teacher offers them half a dozen which offer two examples of each: *The Midwich Cuckoos*, *How Many Miles to Babylon*, Cookson's *The Nipper*, Garnett's *Family from One End Street*, Jill Paton Walsh's *Fireweed* and Cleavers' *Where the Lilies Bloom*. (She has read only two of them herself, scanned two more, and heard much talk of the others from pupils.) The process requires attention to individuals, a willingness to admit 'I don't know . . .' and a readiness to accept that it is bound to be hit and miss. Once it gets going, however, the feedback from the class will give the teacher a vast store of knowledge of what books are about.

Keeping track of such individualized reading is no harder than keeping records of work with a reading scheme: each pupil holds a Personal Reading Inventory and a three-weekly time is given over to updating it. But there has to be a way of ensuring that children have read what they say they have read, and that cannot be done orally, but where the reading is done in class there is much to be said for simply observing what page each child has reached now and again, and recording it. Some children will want to publicize a 'good read', and time should be set aside for this. Asking children to write out the plot is a quick way to make a burden and a bore out of all reading: much better to ask them to answer a question that can apply to all the books in use, such as:

> Choose a character who is not the main one in the story and describe him, remembering that I might not know the story. Then say what actions and events show what he is like, and whether or not you liked him.
>
> Describe a turn of events that took you by surprise, explain why it surprised you, and look for the clues that would have alerted you in advance if you had noticed them.
>
> It is important not to make too much work of writing tasks which are mainly to check on homework: even at the age of 14 the place of writing about books needs to remain a modest one, since the imaginative writing and the books themselves matter much more.

## Classroom approaches 4

Thematic work is an obvious alternative to the class reader, and many course books in English are laid out on what purport to be themes. Here a core novel is accompanied with a range of other books for personal reading, and the thematic links emerge in oral work. Jennifer Morris describes in the Open University booklet referred to earlier a thematic treatment with a first year secondary class, using themes like Adventure, People, Animals. For 'Places' her core novel is Nina Bawden's *Carrie's War*, and she rightly says that it would serve equally for themes like Growing-Up, Relationships and so on. The thematic links with the other books listed are apt to be rather abstract, which reflects the very general nature of the themes. With children of aged 12 and under it is helpful to make the themes much more concrete, as a group of teachers did in a Cambridgeshire village college in devising book-boxes for eight forms of entry: from nine boxes in each of two years each class could draw a box for half-a-term. Reading levels down to remedial were catered for and teaching strategies accompanied each box if needed. Themes included Wartime at Home, Adrift at Sea, With and Without Parents, Brothers and Sisters, North American Indians, Dangerous Pets, Long Solo Journeys, and so on. For the able second-former the approach provided an introduction to making comparisons between books on similar topics, while less skilful readers could have the reading-load tailored quietly to their capacities. Other English work might or might not relate to the theme, which respected the variety in classroom style among the teachers.

To define thematic approaches rigidly as relating only to fiction is pedantic, and themes which rest on collections of books including non-fiction are just as common and just as useful, though they are usually known as book-based projects. The core novel will be from the school stock but the supplementary books may well come from a school library service. I have seen striking examples over a wide range of ages and topics. A fourth year class of juniors did Air Raids, using Rees' *The Exeter Blitz* and (surprisingly but with marked success) Hersey's *Hiroshima*. A first year secondary class doing integrated humanities devoted three weeks for all three subjects to Freedom, using Paula Fox's remarkable novel *Slave Dancer*. A second year secondary class in an ethnically mixed area tackled Relations head on, using Farrukh Dhondy's *East End at your Feet*. (There are accounts of other teachers using the first and last of these themes in the Open University booklet. That on Race illustrates very well how small-group discussion can be structured to head off the otherwise destructive influence of the classroom lout. John Seely deals with the same point in another article there too.) Book-based projects can clearly vary a great deal, but at minimum they entail a class study of the core book and some discussion of it, individual reading of two or more books on the same theme or topic, and some written contribution from the pupils which brings them together, whether in imaginative writing or formal review or some other format.

Thematic and project approaches are both perfectly proper ways of organizing English work and very useful ways of harnessing the expertise of teachers in other subject fields. The book-box on North American Indians was the brainchild of a geographer who found herself enjoying Ruth Underhill's wonderful novels set in Indian tribal culture. Many a history teacher has devised splendid English projects on Roman Britain, Arthurian England, Elizabethan London and so on. Such project work both benefits from talk between colleagues and provides a useful basis for exchanging ideas.

## Where to begin?

I have outlined four main approaches to the main task of putting the class and personal reading of a group on a rational, ordered basis. There is no point in suggesting that one of them is better than the others. I know which of them I could make work successfully in the classroom myself, but colleagues joining a department that used my preferred approach would either have to adopt it (and so perhaps compromise with their own preferences) or use one of their own choice (and so compromise the unity of the department). Such compromises only fudge the issues if they are made without open professional discussion: English is that sort of subject. The commitment of the teacher is quite as vital as the motivation of the pupil, and is worth sacrifices to get. In practice, though, most schools will have an existing custom which the beginner will be wise to fall in with while developing ideas and materials and reasons for striking out in those individual ways which make English teaching the splendid work it can be.

This chapter has mentioned many children's novels in passing, but has expressed views about only a few of them. That is because it is indispensable for teachers to develop their own tastes and reach first-hand judgements. For those readers who have no other way of knowing where to start, here are some suggestions. They are by no means 'best buys' or Desert Island Reads: some will prove tedious, some even outright infuriating, but they will give an idea of the scope and quality of the literature that has overtaken the old choice between classics and rubbish.

**For teachers of children aged 9 and 10**
Ted Hughes *The Iron Man* (Faber)
C. S. Lewis *The Lion, the Witch and the Wardrobe* (Puffin)
Gene Kemp *The Turbulent Term of Tyke Tiler* (Faber, Puffin)
Clive King *Stig of the Dump* (Puffin)
E. B. White *Charlotte's Web* (Puffin)

**For teachers of children aged 11 and 12**
Nina Bawden *Carrie's War* (Puffin)
Frances Hodgson Burnett *The Secret Garden* (Puffin)
Leon Garfield *John Diamond* (Kestrel)
Philippa Pearce *Tom's Midnight Garden* (Puffin)
Ian Serraillier *The Silver Sword* (Puffin)

**For teachers of children aged 13 and 14**
Alan Garner *The Owl Service* (Collins, Fontana Lions)
John Gordon *The House on the Brink* (Puffin)
Joan Lingard *Across the Barricades* (Puffin)
Jill Paton Walsh *The Dolphin Crossing* (Puffin)
Robert Westall *The Machine Gunners* (Puffin)

And, finally as a set of books which even specialists disagree about, and therefore provide excellent material on which to develop an independent taste:

Betsy Byars *The Midnight Fox* (Puffin)
Alan Garner *The Stone Book* (Collins)
Rosa Guy *The Friends* (Puffin)
Esther Hautzig *The Endless Steppe* (Puffin Plus)
Penelope Lively *The Ghost of Thomas Kempe* (Piccolo)
Jan Mark *Thunder and Lightnings* (Puffin)
Jan Needle *My Mate Shofiq* (Fontana Lions)
Susan Sallis *Sweet Frannie* (Heinemann)
Rosemary Sutcliff *The Lantern Bearers* (Oxford)
John Rowe Townsend *A Foreign Affair* (Kestrel)

Chapter 4

# Development in writing

It is easy enough to put a composition topic on the blackboard and tell the class to write on it. It is not so easy to be happy with the results. Unless your class is gifted, and has been well taught in the previous year or two, they will be depressing. In the short-run there will be cases of 'Please, Miss, I can't think of anything to say.' A number of the children will write only a few lines. Much of what the class writes will be dreary and derivative. In the long-run the class will lose interest in writing, and the teacher will lose the most rewarding part of all work in English.

A class of children who have been successfully led into writing at the top of their bent is a fascinating spectacle, worth watching very closely. The skills of leading them to write are not very difficult to acquire, but how to apply them most productively needs some insight into the way children's writing can develop and change in the years from 9–14. The patterns of development, the signs of growth to watch out for, logically come before the teacher's response, so this chapter is devoted to those issues. Chapter 5 will deal with teaching strategies.

Children begin writing with only the haziest of notions about how it all works. Their early problems are with handling the pencil, shaping the letters, getting them on the lines. The later equivalents of these problems do not disappear by the age of 9: children need as much supervision of their handwriting, correction of silly posture, firmness about the school's chosen style, as at any earlier age. By the age of 10 most children should be converting to writing in pen, a fibre-tip being preferable to a ball-point, and the need to insist on adequately legible script endures throughout the secondary school. Most of these matters are part of physical and muscular change, perhaps overlooked too easily in the massive changes taking place in other aspects of children's writing, which form the main substance of this chapter.

Relatively few children by the age of 9 can write continuous prose that matches adult expectations of fluency and clarity. But a majority can come to do so, and many by the age of 14 are writing prose of some complexity. How has that development come about? The earliest attempt to answer that question was numerical: researchers counted the number of words in each sentence or the length of the words or both, and looked at how the results related to age. It proved an exercise in the obvious: younger children wrote shorter sentences with fewer long words, older children wrote longer sentences with more long words. More sophisticated studies tested out the idea that the grammatical and other technical properties of writing would change measurably over an age-span. This method had shown the detailed ways in which scientific writing, for example, differed from ordinary writing, but it is very costly to use. While a great deal of work has been done on the study of linguistic variety, the combination of interest, financing and technical expertise necessary to apply it to the development of writing has not been forthcoming.

A rather different attempt to assess the development of writing ability used an analytical scheme of types of writing, applied only to secondary aged pupils. The London Institute of Education project on the Written Language of 11-18 year olds (1966–71) developed a complex set of categories which was then used to classify many hundreds of scripts. The formal results were not very happy: a high proportion of the scripts had to be classified into a single category, suggesting that the analytical scheme did not match realities. But the project established four fundamental points:

**1**   The development of writing skills cannot be treated simply as changes in vocabulary and sentence organization: it is integrally related to the wider growth of personality.

**2**   The development is uneven between different kinds of writing: the same pupil will write quite mature stories and undeveloped prose in argument in the same month, and even vice versa.

**3**   Development does not seem to follow chronological age in any linear or consistent way.

**4**   One of the key variables is the writer's developing sense of the audience he is writing for.


## The Crediton Project

In the late 1970s a small team led by Andrew Wilkinson based at Exeter University, made another attempt on the problem. They began by setting aside the London team's categories of writing, and reverted to a form of the traditional set of narrative, description, exposition, argument. They also decided to focus on the age-range from 7–13, on the common-sense basis that those years would provide more obvious evidence of change. The traditional categories needed to be modified for that age-range, of course: the set became narrative, autobiographical, explanatory/descriptive, and argument. This in turn gave the research team a set of tasks for the children to write about. The findings are set out in a very readable book, and lie behind much but not all of this chapter. In reaching them, the Exeter team drew on four main categories of development which operate on and can be seen in all four categories of writing: stylistic, cognitive, affective and moral. The examples they quote give abundant support for the view that how we see the world affects how we write about it but that the reverse is also true – how we write about it affects our perceptions of it. So, too, how we write can dam up or liberate the feelings we have about the world, with obvious effects on those feelings in each case. And our state of moral development interacts with our state of writing development in similar ways. So in teaching writing we are not just teaching a skill: we are changing the pupil's consciousness.

That may sound like a rather grandiose claim: 'changing the pupil's consciousness' does not really fit what most of us recall as a tedious part of a tedious subject. But a growing number of teachers have found in the last few years that it is not confined to children: it has been their personal experience too. Numerous groups of teachers have been working on writing, not by talking about it but by doing it. Originating in the USA under the name of the Bay Area Project, it has acquired other forms in England, where many in-service training courses for English teachers include long sessions devoted to writing. They reveal something impossible to understand if you only hear about it: that writing can be much more than simply recording events on paper, and can help the writer to put experience in order, come to terms with failure or trouble, interpret complex feelings to oneself, make very strong emotions more manageable, and much else. All these things can happen in ways that the writer had no conscious intentions about when he began. They bring home the lesson that for the writing to happen at all may be far more important than any mere teacher's assessment of it. It seems to set going the process of letting the writer feel his way round experience at a pace he would not give it in any other part of life. Bringing a class of younger secondary children or adolescents to do this and watching the outcome can be a stirring experience. It is only part of the task of the teacher, but it is the essential part. The other part is contributory, but because the purely linguistic development seems to be greatest before the age of 14, it is the teacher in the middle years whose work in the nuts-and-bolts area of language is influential.

The conclusion that linguistic development is largely complete by the age of 14 reflects a number of investigations. Harold Rosen investigated this issue in connection with his research on the writing of 15 and 16 year olds, and found the performance of a number of quite competent writers actually deteriorated. My own investigations have shown, at least to my own satisfaction, that Advanced Level students in the sixth form may acquire the technical vocabulary of a subject but are still using at 18 the sentence patterns and ways of organizing meaning they used at 13. I have also found that boys of 14–16 who are aiming at CSE in English show a steady reversion from command of written-language forms back to a spoken-language style unless they feel they have a chance of a Grade 1 result. None of this ought to surprise secondary English specialists, but the implications for the years before 14 are serious: moral and social awareness, or the response to and expression of feeling may develop after about 14, and in most children clearly do so, but the language forms available to handle their expression may not change very much. The programme of work up to 14, therefore, has a vitally important part in the pupil's later achievement.

The conclusion has to be that the programme of English teaching needs to balance substance and skills. But we should be in no doubt about their relative priority. The thousands of primary school pupils now blinding their parents with science and talking glibly about floppy discs and interfacing and RAMs are evidence that humans learn the vocabulary they want to learn. Children spell and punctuate well for teachers who expect them to do so and will not accept shoddy work. In one sense, skill deficiencies are easy meat, at least until they have been left so long as to have become deeply ingrained bad habits. Even so, there are developmental patterns to look for in the acquisition of skills as well as in the growing command of writing, in what I propose to call 'meaning management'. But there is no way that young people can be taught to manage their meanings merely by being taught the skills. You cannot teach children to write by stringing spellings and punctuation and grammar lessons together like beads on a string: the beads will prove wooden and the string an illusion.

## What to look for – development in managing meanings

All of us can be deceived by surfaces. A 9 year old wrote this:

> The pint of playing darfts is to moove yor peaces, you have to take yor opponint peaces and moove yor ones up into kweens.
>
> Tom (aged 9)

At first glance this is heavy with error: seven mis-spellings in two dozen words and a number of sad lapses of 'grammar'. But how many children aged 9 can stand back from their topic far enough to start 'The point of x is...'? How many can convey that the game needs two players, using pieces which take those of the opposition and become queens? If all the teacher does with this kind of writing is to give vent to irritation at the surface errors, how will Tom develop to the point reached by Kevin? He is less than a year older:

> You play draughts on a board having eight squares each way alternate black and white. Each player has twelve pieces shaped like a thick 10p coin, the one with the white pieces puts them on the black sqaures nearest to him. The black pieces go on the white sqaures on the other side.
>
> Kevin (aged 10)

This has the same property of standing back, trying to help the reader in an orderly way, very different from this:

> Boys play crikt they hit a ball with a bat and then you run.
>
> Jenny (aged 8)

There is movement from absorption with the immediate object and with the self as observer of it, to recognition of the needs of the reader. But the child of 9 who writes like Jenny is one kind of problem, while the child of 14 who does so is another. The former is likely to grow out of such egocentricity, assuming the reader will fill the gaps, while the latter is expressing boredom and rejection rather than mere incompetence.

Tom arranges his meanings chronologically, and, more obviously, so does Jenny. Kevin is using a different principle: he starts with a section on the board and pieces, goes on to how they are arranged, and (in the unquoted part of his piece) how the moves are made. This is a classifying treatment, whether the writer is conscious of it or not. Tom, on the other hand, is not yet aware that What You Need and How You Play are different parts of his topic. Sometimes this awareness seems fresh in the wording:

> Draughts is a board game. You need a board marked with black
> and white squars eight each way and twelve pieces in each coloure.
> Black pieces go on white squrs and white on black ones. A piece
> takes if it can jump diagnaly foreward over another one.
>
> Cathy (aged 11)

Kevin and Cathy show more, however, than a waning egocentricity. Tom lacks the terms *black* and *white*. This may be 'weak vocabulary' but is much more likely to be a lack of awareness of the reader and his needs: Tom's problem is with the game rather than the reader. Again, Tom's sentence patterns do not help his communication, whereas Kevin is much further ahead in this respect. Cathy, however, can cut her material up very helpfully. She can do this partly because she can do more than just separate her material into segments (called sentences): she can make the segments hang together afterwards. How this is done we shall return to later in this chapter.

By the end of the 9–14 phase, most children should be able to improve on this quality of writing, but the visual image the children can keep in mind when writing makes a great deal of difference: draughts is easier to describe than Ludo because it is so readily visualized, but both games are spatially static. How to tie a tie or a shoelace, by contrast, is a spatial nightmare that almost defies written definition.

A further strand of development in the management of meanings concerns feeling and its expression. The account by Wilkinson and his colleagues of the Crediton Project findings is particularly acute about this. Children of 7 or 8 can be asked to describe some dramatic or terrible event in their own lives and will do so without a trace of perceptible feeling. They are aware of the quality of the event but cannot manage the inclusion of how they and others felt about it. For example:

> The day my Grandad died we got home from school and Mum sat
> us down for tea at the table and said not to eat yet she had
> something to tell us. Our Grandad died from a hart attack and she
> would be away at the fewnrle for a day and Grandma was coming
> to stay and might stay a long time.
>
> Barry (aged 9)

Even to acknowledge the feeling at all is a step forward, and to distinguish between one's own feelings and other people's is a further stage. To be aware of the difference between the various feelings in the story and the feelings of the reader is a further stage yet. The 12 year old author of this story was being rather precocious:

> You will not like this story, but it happened, and my friend and me
> got mixed up in it and we didn't like it either.

The story went on to relate how the writer's mother, living alone with three children in a rural cottage, had encountered an escaped prisoner but remained very cool-headed:

> 'Ah, yes. You will be wanting food, I suppose.'
> 'No, clothes.' The prisoner's voice struck her as strangely calm.
> She did not know whether to be scared or reassured.
> 'Clothes', he repeated, 'And not Sunday best, either.'
> She looked at him, he was a big man. 'There hasn't been a man in this house for seven years. I'm afraid you're out of luck.' She had to fight down the temptation to sound pleased.

Pat (aged 12)

What is precocious in this writing in a 12 year old is not only the standing back to spell out the participants' feelings, but also the management of those feelings through the viewpoint of the main character. Moreover the mother exists not in relation to the writer but as an independent character mediated to us without benefit of family connections. In less developed work the feelings of a story's participants are less clear, often less attended to or reported for us to note, and at earlier stages may not be admitted at all, except as the unavoidable implications of the events set down.

We have looked at four ways in which young writers learn to manage their meanings. They move from egocentric vision to an outlook where another person, usually the intended reader, is recognized. They move from merely chronological organization of content to one where some sort of order or classification is imposed. They learn to segment previously undifferentiated blocks of meaning into sentences which they become able to control without losing their useful separateness. And they become able to include elements of feeling which in time they control and even turn to narrative use. None of these changes can be tied down to a particular age or stage: children grow in these respects with infinite variety. Nor will they necessarily fix themselves as permanent gains: children leap forward and slip back into old ways, in their writing as well as in their reading choices. But these patterns are regular enough and visible enough to offer some clues to teachers about how to 'read' their pupils' prose.

## How language changes

In outlining ways in which children learn to manage meanings, I have looked at aspects which relate to the organization of whole texts. There is another perspective, because these changes are also attended by some identifiable changes in the texture of the language employed. In setting them out I am not suggesting that the meanings and their expression are separate: merely, some readers will find one a more helpful way into the topic than the other, alternative ways of looking at the same thing.

Children aged 9 are not, on the whole, particularly skilful in showing relationships between the events they describe in their stories. Here are some pieces from the work of a class of 9 year olds asked to write about an injured animal.

> My dad was in the gardin and saw a dog, it was limping. He went down the path and picked the dog up and looked at it. He pulled a thorn out of its foot then it left.
>
> Tanya (aged 9)

> A leopard went hunting. One day it sented a gazell, it ran away as fast as it could but its leg was hurt and it went slower and the leopard got it.
>
> Wendy (aged 9)

> My friend's pony is called Tomboy, it is grey all over and lives mostly in a paddock. One day last holidays we brought it in to saddle up and couldn't. Tomboy had a sore in the middle of his back and it would be painful to ride him. We telephoned the vet and took Tomboy back to the paddock with a saddle cloth over him and could not ride him for three weeks.
>
> Karen (aged 9)

Mere length, as we saw, signals nothing: Karen may write more than twice as much as Wendy, but what matters is how, not how much. Here is a child aged 12 on much the same theme:

> Ebenezer, always known in our family as Neezer, is a Siamese cat with a very high opinion of himself. He has a pale creamy body and the darkest brown head, feet and tail. Like most cats he is extremely neat and clean, and most particular about his appearance. Anything on his body that doesn't belong there will be removed sooner or later, with the help of sharp teeth and a tongue like sandpaper. One day Mum was doing the ironing, and Neezer stretched out on the floor under the ironing board because that is where the sun was. Something made Mum drop the iron, and it fell flat on Neezer's marvelous brown tail, and not even his quick reactions could stop a nasty burn . . .
>
> Maria (aged 12)

Here the management of cause-and-effect is not only explicit, but also organized. Wendy's gazelle has or receives an unexplained injury to its leg, and the causal link between that and its being caught is left for the reader to infer. Maria, on the other hand, has told us already that keeping any kind of dressing on the cat's burned tail is going to be hard work. Tanya's father presumably knows that the dog went away without limping, but we do not hear the result of his attention. Karen, too, though she writes at twice the length of Wendy or Tanya, cannot do better in managing cause-and-effect than a full stop after 'and couldn't'. (In passing, notice the distanced effect of Maria's 'Like most cats', telling us she is in control and we shall enjoy the consequences.)

A second pattern of development in the texture of language written by this

45

age-group concerns the treatment of speech-like material and its steady assimilation to the norms of written language. Compare the piece by Tanya quoted above with this:

> My ma was down our garden and found a bird, it had a gammy wing and coudernt fly so she done it in.
>
> Ken (aged 9)

It is tempting to dismiss this as merely 'colloquial' or 'slang'. The trouble with that treatment is twofold. It does not help the child's self-esteem to have what to him is his natural way of speaking dismissed as unacceptable. And it may deflect the teacher from the real problem, which is not so much how to get rid of slang as how to help Ken and his like adopt and engage with the style of written language. The central need for such children is to acquire usable models of writing, but Ken is not just a case of slow development: he is very probably starved of exposure to good models through being a poor reader. Most children, in any case, need help in learning the formal aspects of written language, and the help has to start in the reading curriculum.

A third source of distress to teachers of this age-group, and of some headaches later on, is concord. For example,

> Dan and me was going round ours and just as we'd come in my house we saw . . .
>
> Bert (aged 9)

Concords may be of number (broken in *Dan and me was*), of tense (broken in *was going . . . had come*) or of person (threatened in *ours . . . my*). Correct concords are among the layman's favourite yardsticks of what he calls good English, the kind of minor error that draws forth the wrathful charge of 'bad grammar' from adults who think nothing of saying 'A number of people are . . .'. This fact reflects the brevity of our educational history: those with social aspirations in Britain have only quite recently felt free from the need to acquire carefully correct speech. Until recently, regional accents where false concords could be quite normal would be criticized or a source of embarrassment, and being caught out in one of their habits was a grave social error. (The same holds for dialect itself and of course for other languages, as Emlyn Williams's account of the despised status of the Welsh of his own childhood confirms.) In addition, of course, 'correct' English was universally held to be written English, and while we do not hold this view with such force as in the past we may not have noticed a consequence of that very welcome change.

If the objection to false concords is that they do not belong in written language, they are not the only feature of spoken language with that characteristic. The adult community is ceasing to treat as incorrect many usages by children which are in fact spoken-language usages, so schools have an increased duty to spell out where the boundary lies and what the characteristics of written language are. This has nothing to do with disvaluing the child's own spontaneity: even that spontaneous language has been learned, and in any case no teacher refrains from forbidding infants to swear at her in

Draughts is a board game. You need a board of eight squares in each direction, alternately black and white. Each player has twelve pieces. The player with the black pieces puts them on the white squares and the other player does the opposite. A piece takes one of the other player's pieces if it can jump diagonally forwards over it and land in a space. If it can jump more than one piece by going another jump in the same move, it takes extra pieces. A piece that gets to the other player's back row becomes a queen. That is, you put a spare piece on top of it and it can move backwards as well as forwards. The game is finished when one side has taken all the other side's pieces.

*Figure 3 An example of how continuous prose derives part of its continuity from links between sentences. The figure traces only some of the many links established by reference, repetition etc.*

case it harms their spontaneity of expression. Mere telling is not enough: many children need the help of planned and sustained work on 'translating' expressions common to their own speech into their acceptable equivalents in writing. Such work can readily cover problems with concords if the need is there, but the majority of children will acquire the norms of written English about concord if they are given sufficient exposure to good writing.

Fourthly, one of the major contrasts between young people's writings and those of adults is in the way the segments, usually the sentences, are made to hang together to form a whole continuous text. Cathy, whose work on draughts I quoted on page 43, went through it with her teacher and re-wrote it like this:

> Draughts is a board game. You need a board of eight squares in each direction, alternately black and white. Each player has twelve pieces. The player with the black pieces puts them on the white squares and the other player does the opposite. A piece takes one of the other player's pieces if it can jump diagonally forwards over it and land in a space. If it can jump more than one piece by going another jump in the same move, it takes extra pieces. A piece that gets to the other player's back row becomes a queen. That is, you put a spare piece on top of it and it can move backwards as well as forwards. The game is finished when one side has taken all the other side's pieces.

I said above that her readiness to cut her material up into sentences reflects her confidence that she can hold the separate parts together. How this is done can be seen by looking at Figure 3 (see above) which traces the connections most of us take for granted.

Being able to segment one's writing into sentences is a major advance. Going beyond this is a much bigger one. A series of sentences enables a writer to separate a from b from c from d and still show a-b-c-d as a coherent sequence. Being able to organize meanings into paragraphs as well as sentences permits far more complexity: it enables the writer to separate A from B from C from D, and in doing so to arrange $a_1$-$a_2$-$a_3$-$a_4$ as constituent parts of A without disturbing B-C-D. The kind of writing that happens when this change needs to emerge can be seen in the next example, by a boy aged 11 or 12:

> When I grow up I want to be a vet, I don't mind the blood and that but will have to get used to hurting animals sometimes I suppose but I will like helping them get better (1). I want to have a surgery with stainless steel tables and a big waiting room and a sign by the door at the front (2). I expect I will need a partner to help with the work, we could share the weekend calls, he will do the farm animals and I will do the small ones and pets but I might get used to cows and pigs by then (3). I will have to go to university for a long time first, I don't want to spend six years at college but I will probably have to and I know it's hard to get in (4). I will want to have two dogs of my own to go with me on the rounds and when I go home I might be able to look after my mother's three cats and parrot (5).
>
> John (aged 11 or 12)

I have numbered the sentences, and a careful look at each one suggests that they are all very 'heavy', very densely packed with blocks of meaning which in adult prose would each have a separate sentence to itself. What holds each sentence together is an underlying unity of topic:

| | | | |
|---|---|---|---|
| **1** | The vocation | **4** | Training |
| **2** | The premises | **5** | The domestic side |
| **3** | The partnership | | |

In adult writing such a series of meaning-clusters would be organized into five paragraphs, each made up of three to six sentences. When a child masters this organizational use of paragraphing, as distinct from a purely formalistic layout notion imposed regardless of meanings and their shape, a great deal more happens besides a change of appearance. Here is an example cited by Kress, from a writer aged about 12 who has only just made this step:

BEAKED WHALES

1    The Beaked Whales live out in mid-ocean, where the tasty squid are found. Squid, it seems, provide most of their meals. Men do not know much about their family because even the scientists who study whales have seen very few Beaked Whales. Generally
5    members of this family have long, narrow snouts or 'beaks'. They have very few teeth, just one or two on each side of the lower jaw, and these sometimes poke out like small tusks.

      The largest of this family is the Baird's Beaked Whale. It grows to 42 ft. in length. Most beaked whales range between 15 and 30 ft.
10    The Bottlenose gets to be about 30 ft. long, and its cousin known as Cuvier's Beaked Whale grows to about 26 ft.

      Cuvier's Whale is rarely seen, though it is believed that it lives in all oceans. It is unusual in colour, so if you should see one you

should be able to recognize it. Most whales have dark grey backs
15    and pale undersides. Cuvier's Beaked Whale instead has a light back
and a dark grey underside, and two small tusk-teeth poke up
outside the mouth of the males.

    Bottlenose is even more odd. You may probably see one
travelling in a small school of ten or twelve whales.

As Kress notes, the paragraphs here (beginning at lines 1, 8, 12 and 18) 'encode significant topical segments of the whole text' much as did the sentences in the previous example. The effect of being able to use the paragraphing for this function (marking out the major topic-portions) is to relieve the sentences of the burden. The sentences can then abandon their breathless pursuit of major topic. Each sentence can concentrate on its own (minor) topic, can take its time and feel secure within the wider framework. Way is thus opened for a greater variety of sentence form and more varied patterns of linkage between sentences. Attempts to teach these variations independently of the expressive urge behind the need for them have not been much of a success: it seems that if children are going to learn to manage meanings, they first have to have the meanings to manage.

## Processed speech as narrative

Finally we should return to one underlying feature of the contrast between the pieces by Barry and Pat that were quoted on pages 43 and 44. This is the management of people speaking and thinking. Consider the class of 10 year olds who went to an air museum and heard their guide say:

    'Now there is Concorde: look at it carefully.'

That speech-event appeared in their accounts of the day in a number of guises:

    He said there is Concorde and to look at it carefully.
    He said Concorde was there and we should look at it carefully.
    He said we would see Concorde and could look at it close up.
    He said Concorde would be there and we were to look at it.
    There's concord he said look at it carefully.
    Our teacher obviously thought Concorde was a great thing for the
    museum to have, and so did the guide.

What effect, we may wonder, will diligent teaching of the punctuation of direct speech have on this variety? The words do not have to be written in full punctuational form for them to be understood as quoted from life, but insisting rigidly on direct speech properly punctuated could suppress other meanings the writer wants to build in, as one girl showed:

    There was Concorde, he said, in a tone that meant would we please
    do him the honour of looking at it closely.

We expect these distinctions between directly quoted speech, reported speech, and what Kress calls processed speech. In literature they are crucial to texture: in the passage from *Mrs Frisby* quoted on page 78 we are unsure whether the state of the food supply is the author's account of fact or Mrs Frisby's grim observations reported, and we relish the ambiguity. The distinctions between direct, reported, and processed speech are a major element in this piece, written by a capable girl of just 10.

FIRE DISASTER AT CHILDREN'S HOSPITAL

At one forty Tuesday afternoon fire broke out in the kitchen of St Andrews hospital. It all started as the cook went to serve some chips at the table. She had been careless and had left the tea–cloth by the oven. When the cook came back the tea cloth had caught on fire and was spreading all over the floor. The cook got very frightened and when I spoke to her later on this evening she said, 'I thought my life had ended!' But she was wrong. She put on the fire alarm and started bustling every-one out of the door. Meanwhile, as nurse Winters has just pointed out, on the top floor they were panic stricken. The fire brigade came a little later on. Mr Barns said that the fire was spreading fast but it wouldn't have happened if Mrs Whitewater (the cook) hadn't been so careless. Mr Barns (the fire engine driver) was very cross with Mrs Whitewater and said 'She wasn't fit to be a cook.' Most of the children had escaped but sixteen were trapped on the top floor. There was nurse Winters on this floor she was very scared herself as she had already told me. Then she had a brainwave and started knotting strong blankets together. She requed sixteen children and later on will be collecting an OBE from the queen herself. There was 1,000 pounds worth of damage done not including the equipment and builders are busy rebuilding St Andrews hospital.

This piece also provides a revealing study in the ambitious but uncertain use of tense. One might note how the insistent demand for quotation marks on all instances of speech would deprive this girl of the distinction she probably wants to make between something spoken out loud to all and sundry and something said in confidence to the writer. It was a wise teacher who refrained from making any overt corrections on it.

# Chapter 5

# Teaching writing

Running through the previous chapter, appearing in several different forms, was a theme: 'They first have to want to mean.' Unless children have been provided with many possible things to say or think, they will revert to the oft-repeated cry 'Please, Miss, I can't think of anything to say.' That is a situation to deal with not when it occurs but long in advance. The related theme about skills for writing, at any level, was that teaching isolated skills would not of itself help children to become better writers, although it may help some adults. Also, the patterns and traces of development in children's writing are consequences, not targets: the objectives for good teaching have to be those of the best work the children can achieve, not the means whereby the teacher recognizes it.

## What *is* creative writing?

There have been two main approaches to teaching writing in the English school tradition. The older one was the weekly 'composition', modelled ultimately on the literary essay. It became part of the weekly routine of grammar schools in the days before any other kind of secondary education, from there became enshrined in the traditional course book, and so we find even today many primary school classes teach English with a little bit of grammar, a little bit of spelling, a little bit of 'comprehension' and a little bit of writing, week after week. This tradition is of very little use to most children of any age, though it may pass for adequate among the able, and it is uninspiring even for them. The alternative originated in the 1930s and in the late 1960s became influential, especially through the advocacy of David Holbrook's *English for the Rejected*. 'Creative writing', to give this approach its usual label, became the dominant orthodoxy wherever English specialist teachers were trained, and its effect on practice in the schools was liberating and potent.

The defining features of 'creative writing', or rather of the teaching approach which seeks that, are:
1   The teacher may suggest the theme or topic, but each pupil is encouraged to treat it in an individual, personal way.
2   The theme or topic may take the form either of words on the board or of event or experience or stimulus (such as a piece of music or a short piece of writing). The topic, if then put into words, becomes a label for or link to the stimulus.
3   Pupils are encouraged to write from direct experience or on the basis of something they find intrinsically interesting.
4   The use of literature which exhibits free use of form and compression or intensity of feeling encourages writing that does the same.

**5**   The approach can lead to a dialogue between what pupils offer and the teacher's responses that creates an atmosphere of mutual trust. This in turn sets the writing free to be adventurous and sometimes deeply personal.

This general approach obviously suits children and adolescents of 13 or 14 and over better than those in the younger age-bracket. It can be of great value in helping young people wrestle with the conflicts of adolescence, and correspondingly where younger children face such problems too, but that cannot be a main argument for using it. Some teachers adopt the full creative writing approach in middle schools successfully, but they tend to be specialists who can get round the problems of their pupils' more limited range of experience and less developed scope of feeling. Most teachers of children aged 9–14 have to adapt the approach because of the nature of the children, and because the rest of their curriculum is in their charge rather than under a set of subject specialists. Whatever the adaptation, however, two features of the creative writing approach have influenced writing work at all levels:

**6**   Children are encouraged, and occasionally obliged, to regard their first writing on a topic as a draft, which can be revised, modified, improved, even rewritten completely – and in that way is much closer to normal adult writing.

**7**   The teacher's response is much more than a mere mark: discussion with the author, questions about intention, suggestions for improvement, encouragements to develop a line further, and so on.

### The conditions for good writing work

The necessary adaptation of the creative writing approach with children aged 9 and upwards preserves several features of the model. The conditions in which good work usually emerges are:

**1**   The classroom has a plentiful supply of good models and examples which are used all the time to show what is possible and what is permissible.

**2**   The writing work needs a plan, and the development of each main writing task within it needs a planned build-up.

**3**   The way in which the topics are worded usually needs to be more concrete and specific, while children who want to be ambitious are set free from such wordings if they want to be.

**4**   For the great bulk of the time allocated to writing, the work is done in silence.

**5**   The teacher herself is an active participant in the work.

Each of these conditions calls for a brief filling out.

**1   Models and examples**   The classroom library should include between 20 and 30 books of prose and poetry likely to be of interest to children of the relevant age. The work of selecting these only has to be done once, and is itself a crucial part of the training of any teacher who hopes to do English well. There are two needs to serve in making your selection: to bring together a wide variety of examples, which include work by children as well as adults, and to identify no more than one or two anthologies to be bought in by the school in a class set of 20 or 30 copies. (It matters very much that the class have a 'bank' of pieces they all know as well as an 'account' of pieces they have found as individuals.) Some anthologies suit a wide range, and others run in series: those by Barry Maybury in the Oxford list are outstanding examples of the one, while Geoffrey Summerfield's poetry collection *Junior Voices* (Penguin) comes in four volumes that are not graded and have many pieces by children. These books are for dipping into, sometimes for 'Will you find a poem you would like to read to the class', sometimes for the teacher to draw on in developing a stimulus. The need for a large stock of them reflects the fact that children's tastes will change over the year, and provides a greater number of ideas for the teacher and the children to use – pattern and concrete poems are cases in point.

**2   Plan the work and plan the tasks**   The teacher does need to have some idea where she is going over the school year in the writing work. One framework could be developed from the four categories of writing looked at by the Crediton Project: the programme needs, we might say, to include narrative, autobiography, description and argument, so the tasks should ring the changes on these four; but we might well add that the plan needs to include them in the proportion 3:2:1:1 because equal weighting for all four would make for a rather arid scheme. Each task also needs planning in the sense that there has to be a clear aim in the teacher's mind that her pupils will be writing on a theme she has identified, and she is setting out to base that writing on a planned or guided build-up. It can start from actual events (a headline on the morning news, an episode on the way to school), real experience ('Have any of you been involved in an accident at a zoo?' – but be ready with alternatives if you draw a blank), a literature source, a reading or a record the teacher selects deliberately to make a start to the build-up she wants. The build-up needs to draw out the ideas and reactions of the children, elaborate some of them, show how others can be made use of, and most of them can be written up in a very abbreviated form on the blackboard as an ideas-store. That is probably much more useful than the word-store technique common in writing work with younger juniors, except where technical terms involve spelling difficulties. With children of aged 12 and over the build-up can go further into questions of technique referred to later in this chapter.

**3   Wording the topic**   One of the great enemies of ready writing by children is the one-word essay title. Here are some examples of story titles that arose from good preparatory discussion with children aged 9 which sought to put into words the essence of what they had been talking over:

> Tiny accident with not so tiny results
> The time five things happened on the bus to school
> The day the bed fell on my uncle

The ghost who broke plates in the dishwasher
How I found my father (episode on a family holiday)

It is difficult to strike the right balance between wording a topic so as to support those children who need the help of a very specific target and cramping the style of those who can be more ambitious. Much can be done, however, by the teacher's own intervention when the writing is beginning. (See point 5 below.)

**4   Silence**   There is a widespread misconception that because talk is creative and writing is, ideally, also creative, children should be encouraged to be talkative during writing sessions. There is a place for a limited amount of discussion in pairs about a writing task, but if the build-up has been successful it should not be necessary. After that brief time the regime for writing should be one of silence. The reason, if one needs a reason for such common sense, is that children who write in silence write between three and six times as much as those who are allowed to chatter, and chatterers never discover what they are capable of, any more than do their teachers.

**5   The role of the teacher**   When the writing begins, the teacher will first need to speak briefly with the handful of reluctant writers, those who will find a difficulty in a topic if they can, and need to be helped/steered/pushed round it. Then she will need to visit the distractables, the two or three children in most classes who will find something else to do and will need to be told firmly to get on with the job. By then there will be one or two puzzled faces needing advice, and within 15 minutes there will be a few to be helped whose writing has yet to progress beyond a few lines. The teacher in a writing period is on the move all the time, reminding here, placing a question there, scanning the state of progress all the time, watching the balance between the pupils' span of concentration and the scale of the task they have been set, picking up sensitively the moment for saying, 'Very well: we shall stop the writing now and pick it up again tomorrow.' It is common practice for writing tasks to be set to run to a school bell, but if they were set to run to their natural term they would usually benefit.

## The 9–11 age-range

The majority of writings in this age-range will naturally be stories. Each writer will exhibit particular narrative habits, whatever the topic or build-up. The general aim should be to make sure there is plenty of material to draw on: there is much recall of incident and the beginnings of some ideas about treatment. The specific aim in many cases depends on the narrative habits exhibited by the children. Let us look at each of these aims in more detail.

A very mundane example occurs regularly enough: the class or the school enjoys an outing or visit, to a historic site let us say, or to the seaside, and the visit is milked for all it is worth in environmental studies or whatever other emphasis the trip had. Asked to write a story based on the visit, many children of this age will write three or four sentences on getting ready and getting aboard, two or three about the coach ride out, one sentence on some incident at the other end and one sentence about coming home. What lies behind this painfully frequent inadequacy of writing is now easy to see: the preliminary talk has somehow not reminded them of the sights and sounds and smells of the place they visited, the approach to writing has omitted to give them guidance about shape and balance, and the lack of attention to direct experience has allowed them to let too much pass unobserved. Beyond these problems, the absence of examples and other varieties of writing makes their offerings stereotyped first-we-did-this-and-then-we . . . narrative.

When the children are led to sit up and take notice on their journeys, disposed to see anything and everything that happens to them as potential grist to the writing mill, and ready to use a variety of forms and styles, they will write very differently. A day-trip to the seaside will yield a clutch of poems on things seen – the candy-floss stall, the helter-skelter, sand in one's shoes, limpets sticking like limpets; a group of adventure stories located in the cliffs and caves the writers have actually seen; one or two fantasies about being left behind or lost at sea. This kind of diversity is what the teacher should be looking for, of course, with a wary eye on the writer whose output is restricted to six-line 'poems'. Marking in the narrow sense is beside the point, and response and comment take its place.

Even so, some children will remain in the safety of the stereotyped simple story, and what we need to observe about this is that it is in many cases just that, a safety play: it avoids commitment and self-exposure. There are ways of helping children towards a more committed response to writing, without forcing them into a personal exposure, and if the child's work reveals a distinctive narrative habit one can use it. Here are some good examples from teacher comments on such writings, again in the context of the class visit to the seaside:

> Your stories always start before anything really happens, Darren, and never really get to the real thing. Next time, why not write it as a set of flashbacks, pictures in your mind on the way home?
> But, Mary, you never actually get us there! Please go on a bit: suppose you are sitting in the cafe, tell us what it looked and felt like.
> Yes, John: another of your flat general pictures. For next week's writing would you write a poem or a piece about <u>one</u> thing looked at really closely. A sandcastle or a small patch of beach, no more.
> Thank you, Tina: you have written down the report you gave to Assembly, and it reads very well. But there's no flavour of the town in it. Next week we are trying again, and I hope you can tell one of your stories with the town as the setting, sights and steps and smells and sand-dunes!

At some point, too, children will ask, 'Please, Miss, does it have to be true?'

The best answer is to have forestalled the question by some discussion of how chunks of real events and settings can be made use of in telling stories, and how real people can serve as models for fictional characters.

The heart of the work with children of 9–11, then, is the process of bringing them to 'sit up and take notice' and to make use of their observation. This is slow work, not to be achieved fully even in a whole school year. It cannot be done successfully by formalistic tasks of the 'study this closely and write about it' type: the children have to be engaged in the topic in some way, their personal interest stirred and exploited. That holds whether one uses a formal framework or scheme or not. One well-tried framework is Maybury's widely used book *Creative Writing for Juniors*. His sequence through sense training can become a laboured string of topics instead of a structure, but the suggestions for treatment of topics are numerous and practicable: they have clearly worked.

The dominance of story needs limiting, too. Even at the age of 10 children need to experience the range of varieties of writing, and to develop a repertoire of types. Topic work will give rise to recording and describing, and classroom debate and discussion will lead to some kinds of argument, but it is far better to use real events if one can. For example, a local paper printed a letter from a well known local figure on the laxity of modern schooling and how much better it all was in his day. The class wrote their replies, under the promise that the ten best would be sent. The teacher quietly suggested to the gentleman that if he wanted to write again he select one pupil to address his letter to, and a correspondence followed in which eight pupils took part in turn while the whole class followed every sentence intently. In another school a new class was formed from the incomers whose parents had occupied a large new housing development during the summer. Their teacher was also new to the area, and she found the class very mixed, showing many signs of stress, unpopular with the established children, their mothers unsettled and at a loss, everyone insecure about the new situation. Partly to give the class a unifying focus, the teacher set them to a series of project-type inquiries about the neighbourhood, the nearby market town, the facilities on the new estate, local shops, buses, services, and so on. The picture of isolation at home and lack of contact that came out of all this led to the idea of a class newspaper. Children paired off for writing assignments – news items about the poor drainage and unreliable rubbish collection, factual items about doctors and surgery times, articles about Where Local Buses Go, When the Street Markets Are, Local Supermarkets, Is the Bus into Town a Wise Investment, interviews with the headmaster and (instructively) the school caretaker. The writers elected an editor, who had to decide on page size and who ran a layout morning, when she had to say to several writers, 'Do your own cutting or I'll cut it for you. Save five lines.' With headlines to write, a masthead to design, distribution to organize, and costs to work out and cover, every pupil had a job to do. (The paper was run off by the local secondary school resources department, at cost, and sold for enough pennies to cover.) The enterprise took five weeks from initial field-work to completed copy; children hardly noticed the scale or the skill of the writing that filled the paper, or the immense gain in fluency and clarity that made the second issue two pages longer than the four-page first issue. The teacher saw to it that the class were absorbed in something else before anyone thought about a third issue, but what she remembered best was the ruthless severity shown by the sub-editors to the three laziest writers in the class, one of whom was sent away with the lofty dismissal of, 'Go away and re-write it: we don't want the junk you serve up for Miss!'

Unless a project of this type provides the writers with the material and the treatments necessary for good writing, description and argument work will benefit from preparatory discussion just as much as narrative. Children who are faced with an issue to discuss tend at this age to formulate an attitude and find whatever single contention seems to them to support or justify it. Writing that down leads to very thin results, and the benefits from some rehearsing of the divers attitudes one can adopt and the arguments that apply (or do not, as the case and logic may be) will be particularly obvious.

Possible topics can include: Should School Not be Compulsory, Would Four Terms a Year be Better than Three, Should Everyone have to Belong to a Uniformed Youth Group, and the like. Here again the topics available change in depth as the children become more confident in handling argument: children of 11 can develop sensitive responses to such issues as collective child rearing (on Kibbutz lines) versus the nuclear family, merging ordinary schools and physically handicapped pupils, and the like, but they will have had to learn at an earlier stage about the ordering of arguments one against another and about the ways in which that is put into writing.

## The 12–14 age-range

Much of what has been said about the 9–11 age-range applies here too. For reasons outlined in the previous chapter, this may be for many pupils the optimum phase. After it, many young people undergo changes in attitude and aspiration that serve to restrict or limit their commitment to school in general and writing in particular. In many such cases, the work in English becomes unwitting victim of demoralizing aspersions cast by teachers of other subjects. It is in the 12–14 stage more than any other that writing can most serve as a means to personal development, although it may not be obvious that this is happening. For all these reasons, the formulation of topics and the specification of approach need just as much care as with younger writers, but with a different focus. There are two main ways in which to structure this, and a sound approach in these years will blend the two. One is the enlargement of the writers' sense of audience, and the other is the deliberate use of variation in the persona adopted by the writer. Both are commonplace aspects of adult writing, and with committed pupils can become powerful elements later in the course, but there is a need for them to start earlier.

The simplest start on the notion of audience is the 'Postcard Scheme'. Each pupil has to find a picture postcard of a place known or recently visited. The space available on it for the message is measured and a dummy of it laid out in an exercise book. Groups of four then compete to convey the maximum information in that space within the limits of being grammatical and legible. Stage Two divides the class into pairs. Each pair chooses one card, invents a distinctive but probable recipient, and writes a full, written character-outline of this real or imaginary reader. The pair then have to adapt the previous draft to suit that audience, or provide a new one. The members of the pair, A and B, then become respectively the audience thus addressed (let us say, miserly uncle) and 12 year old writer. B writes his card, and A replies. B writes another card, but A writes back demanding a proper letter. After B has written the requested letter, A devises a set of questions asking for information the cards and letter have left out. If the class is ready for it, the pairs then go back and rewrite the original card(s) so as to include the information later requested. The work needs some discussion of the A roles and how such characters would react, so that their potential is realized without undue exaggeration.

The next step is to move slowly into writing tasks in which the notion of audience is specified with increasing precision. It is both very difficult to bring children of 12–13 to perceive the needs of the reader and peculiarly important to do this. Some audiences can be specified precisely enough to provide a stimulus in itself, if the implications are worked out in the preliminary discussion. Examples include the problems of describing landscape to a person who is colour-blind, but such tasks have an air of artificiality about them by comparison with what is possible after contact with a real instance. The Red Cross will lend wheelchairs to schools so that children can learn by occupying one, or escorting a chair-bound classmate, what the problems are of getting about at home or in their own school – an exercise that reveals things about people and self as well as about building and handicap. I have seen teachers attempt a silence experiment in which everyone acts as if deaf for a time, in preparation for writing to a deaf reader, but this is more demanding than it looks: far better to persuade a handicapped person to talk face-to-face about the handicap and answer questions. Some teachers have found, too, that tasks which are very audience-specific will stimulate pupils who otherwise prove very reluctant writers. For example, one group of three such boys aged 13 were asked to identify three lonely old people, make their acquaintance, and develop the contact by writing to them what they would be interested to read about. The results were astonishing.

These variations on the notion of audience share the attempt to locate real situations in which real people have to live and work, so that children can try to understand and cater for the realities. Some of them involve the discovery that handicap can often be more difficult to observe from outside than to live with. Some of them encourage the development of contacts with people that are unique to each child and private in a way that classroom activity needs to treat with respect. It is facile to suppose that any and every writing by children at this age is equally capable of being posted on the classroom display wall or displayed on an open evening. If the writing programme is achieving one of its objectives, it is providing a channel in which children can write their way through a difficulty, crystallize their thoughts and feelings, even bring them under control. (One child aged 10 wrote a piece called 'The day I killed my

Mum', and readily agreed that it grew out of being furiously angry with her – but they had made it up since.) A consequence of this has to be that we should not share or display our pupils' writing without asking their consent. That surely applies whether the work in question is creative writing or any other sort.

For one of the governing realities about the 12–14 phase is the immense diversification going on in the range and type of the writing asked of young people. Each subject of the curriculum at this level is gradually separating itself off from the others, and one of the main ways in which they do this is by gradually using language in more and more special ways. It is possible to have some mild fun with this, as the teacher did who asked a class of girls aged 13 in a history lesson to dissect a Victorian crinoline and write, not a description of how it was made, but a dressmaking pattern for making a new one. (Here as in most other cases of technical language the best thing a teacher can do with jargon is to ask pupils to imitate an example if they can: deriding it is merely to air one's prejudices.) This progressive differentiation of language in the curriculum leaves English with two kinds of language all its own: fiction, whether in prose or in play form, and poetic language, whether in prose or verse form. The English teacher can very usefully set going some study of language variety by presenting a class with fragments of text lifted from a specific context and inviting the pupils to work out, from the evidence available, what the context of each might be – and the contexts do not all have to be contemporary or even modern. (One of the most successful approaches I have seen to starting the study of Shakespeare with a mixed ability third year class in a secondary school took the form of a series of six sheets of such extracts, studied one a week, where older language styles occurred in each among more modern material.) But the central tasks remain in fictional and poetic writing.

## Fictional writing and poetic writing

By the age of 13, a good proportion of children should be capable of writing short stories of reasonable scale. Before the teacher knows it, though, many such pupils develop all the signs of being bored with story writing. Closer inspection will often reveal that what is really happening is that competent writers are in fact writing the same story over and over again with only the most surface changes of setting and characters. (If their reading is similarly stereotyped, the situation is the more likely.) Looked at in this light, the writing of many classes of second year children in secondary schools, and not a few others, merits some stocktaking about the precise nature of the story-writing challenge put before them. Some of the variations to suggest are obvious: write the story as a flashback in which your narrator tells the story to a frankly incredulous friend; write it as three or four scenes in a play or broadcasting script; write the story rigidly and exclusively as a conversation – and so on. But the simplest approach is to propose careful variation of the persona adopted as the narrator. With bright children this quickly becomes a can-you-fool-me game, in which the trick is to keep the reader guessing as long as possible about the identity of the narrator, or to surprise him with a dénouement about it. With the general run of children of 12 and 13 it can become a very useful device for what we might call stretching the imagination.

For example, it is worth taking the time involved in a preliminary discussion if the task is a calculated challenge such as 'Tell the story of Robinson Crusoe as if you were Man Friday', or some similar treatment of a conventional tale from a very unconventional viewpoint. At first, of course, most children will labour the change: it will take time for them to realize that they do better to keep rather quiet about who is writing, letting it emerge incidentally from clues laid here and there. From this it is a shorter step to the notion that a great deal of fictional and poetic writing rests on the common understanding that the first-person narrator of a story or poem is not automatically to be identified with the author. It is difficult to keep any kind of link going between the development of this insight into literature and its implementation by the children in their writing, and that may not be necessary in any case, but there are some fine examples of poems which show the poet entering into the persona of somebody quite different. Here is Theodore Roethke's *Child on Top of a Greenhouse*:

> The wind billowing out the seat of my britches,
> My feet crackling splinters of glass and dried putty,
> The half-grown chrysanthemums staring up like accusers,
> Up through the streaked glass, flashing with sunlight,
> A few white clouds all rushing eastward,
> A line of elms plunging and tossing like horses,
> And everyone, everyone pointing up and shouting!

The use of a clearly defined narrator-figure can be a great help to developing writers. The fact that it associates clearly with the traditional convention of the unities is accidental, but boys and girls bored with adventure yarns and cops-and-robbers can be faced with some engaging suggestions based on the same ideas. Thus, one can ask a capable writer of age 13 to tell the story of a burglary that went badly wrong in the medium of an exchange of half a dozen letters between the woman who was to have been robbed and a correspondent overseas. A pupil with some degree of learning difficulty in the same class can be asked to relate to the teacher an account of a burglary he has imagined happening at home.

Fictional writing, which is by definition writing that takes liberties with fact, can take the form of narrative prose or of scripted play, and in the same way poetic writing may be in the form of poem or prose. Poetic writing needs ideally to be available to children who want to use it rather than an imposed requirement, but making it available in the first place entails some initial compulsion. Once children know what it involves and what it is capable of, poetic writing can revert to its proper status as an option to take up as and when the writer needs it. This in turn means that the option has to be opened up in the first place and thereafter kept alive, especially if the poetic writing is ever to take the form of poems. Without many good models of the distinctive compression and intensity of feeling that poetry offers, children will fall back on older models of nursery rhymes and hymn forms where a compulsion to rhyme dominates the writing. There are many good models and examples in the anthologies mentioned in this chapter and others listed in the Notes and References (page 121), which nobody ever thought less of because they did not rhyme. Mere 'free verse', however, is a sprawling and undisciplined activity for many children, and help is ready to hand in the form of disciplined practice with specific forms such as Haiku, Tanka, Cinquains and several more. This approach is set out in splendid detail and with obvious fun in Sandy Brownjohn's short book *Does it Have to Rhyme?* (Hodder). A Haiku is a Japanese verse form of three lines, respectively of 5, 7 and 5 syllables. As Sandy Brownjohn says, 'One of the great lessons to be drawn from writing Haiku is that choosing words carefully, to express as much as possible, should be carried over into all writing.' This is not the only way to approach poetic expression, of course, but the need to encourage writing which seeks to express meanings and feelings remains paramount. The only school-age writers who should be encouraged to explore rhyme schemes and metrical forms are those who feel drawn to experiment with them: the alternative is rhythmical chuntering that exactly fits the definition of doggerel.

Poetic writing, then, does not have to rhyme or adhere to a metre, nor even does it have to be laid out on the page as poetry: rather, there is a continuum between the prosaic and the poetical, and this diversity exists within poetic literature as well as in the novel. Much poetic writing, however, depends for part of its effect on its visual shape on the page: to read six four-line stanzas of a poem sets up very firm expectations about the seventh and last such stanza, and rhyme itself is more than a solely phonic affair. This is why the collection of poetry books in each classroom is an integral part of the writing programme, especially the collection which takes in some of the volumes of entries to the Children's Poetry Competition published each year under the title *Children as Writers*.

## I writes like I talks, don' I . . .

One of the central threads in the process of becoming a writer is that the learner has to acquire a steadily greater distancing of the norms of natural speech. Some children absorb this truth as part of learning to read: for them, writing is not only a different medium from speaking, but is one where the norms and peculiarities hang together from a very early stage. Most children are learning the main norms of written English from the middle infant stage to well on into the junior years: it is quite reasonable to expect the learning to spread out over the range from the age of 7–8 to that of 13–14. The norms of standard written English are asserted in many different ways: chiefly through the sustained exposure to written literature that underpins the English curriculum, supported of course by corrections and marking and sometimes by formal exercises devised to deal with particular problems. There has to be some rigour about all this between 9 and 14: afterwards may be too late. What that entails is set out more fully in Chapter 7, with a more specialized note on accent and dialect in Chapter 10.

Chapter 6

# Teaching the catching of spelling

No topic dealt with in this book produces as much argument, embarrassment and sense of failure as spelling. Most of us have childhood memories of grim encounters with English spelling and a majority of us still have the occasional uncertainties. Some adults, including teachers, retain real anxieties about their own spelling throughout life. Perhaps this accounts for our collective inability to register the logic of commonplace facts. The incidence of adult illiteracy is certainly cause for concern, but no authority has put it higher than 6%, which means that over 90% of the population can read and over 80% can read competently. Moreover the great majority of those who can read can also spell. The spelling that so many people have mastered, albeit with problems at the margin for even highly educated people, must therefore be capable of being learned. In order to be learnable it must have some properties of order if not of system. Why in the face of these facts otherwise sensible people believe that our spelling is totally chaotic, or that only spelling reform can save us from disaster, quite passes understanding. If, then, English spelling can be learned, and indeed is learned, it should be possible to identify the stages by which the learning happens. It should also be possible to set out a few principles for an approach to teaching spelling that harmonizes with the system rather than maximizes its admitted irregularities. Those are the tasks of this chapter, which in places will have to be a bit more technical than the rest of the book.

## Preliminary: handwriting

Before we come to spelling itself, a brief note is necessary about handwriting. Most teachers believe, and I share their view, that there is a perceptible association between poor handwriting and bad spelling. By 'good handwriting' I do not mean italic script or any other variety of calligraphy, which is a separate art and one of some value for a school to pursue at the club level. But good handwriting does not just happen: it has to be an objective of systematic teaching over a long period of time. For that very reason, it needs to be the subject of a school policy, one in which individual teachers may have to submerge their personal preferences, because it is essential for children to be taught consistently over several years. Moreover the policy will only work if teachers who are disinclined to drive their pupils submerge that reluctance too: handwriting needs regular and tedious routine practising of letter shapes in along-the-line drills for regularity, repetition to get it right, insistent and often niggling correction about completing a letter shape, or holding the pen, or maintaining a consistent slope. Moreover these disciplines do not stop at any particular age: children of 11 and 12 need them even more than those of 9, because the pressures of the secondary curriculum can make even well-grounded writing styles break down.

There are several perfectly acceptable writing schemes on the market, the best developed among them probably being the Nelson scheme. The most helpful book on the topic is that by Christopher Jarman. All the sound sources agree that copybook approaches are counter-productive. Most experts also make the point that since secondary schools expect the use of pen and ink, children should have made this change by the age of 10; and while a good fountain pen may be on the way to the historical museum, experience with a variety of instruments will help children to see for themselves the deeply destructive effect of ball-point pens on writing styles. (Fibre-tip pens are far better: the minimal resistance between page and tip makes a major difference.)

## Stages in learning

Children acquire their command of spelling over a long period and there is no single way of doing it. There are some identifiable stages in the process, related to what they learn rather than the age or method involved, and these stages do seem to arrive in some kind of order, but any description will make the whole progression look much neater than it can ever be in practice.

The first stage is not primarily one of learning to spell at all, but is the phonic stage in learning to read. It needs to be largely over by the age of 8 or 8½, but shades off into a long process of adjusting the initial phonic knowledge to accommodate the many variants found in spelling as it is encountered in reading. A second stage, which begins long before the first stage is completed, is mainly concerned with the spelling features of two-syllable words (whereas the first stage relates mainly to one-syllable ones). These include **-e** deletion, the change from **-y** to **-i-** and consonant doubling. The stage begins at or soon after the age of 7 and is in full flow for about three years. For some children it will go on for as long again: the child of 12 who has yet to master these features is neither unusual nor backward. The second stage is obviously a prime concern of this chapter. The third stage is chiefly concerned with the formation of complex words, which in English is dominated by a pattern known as affixation. Plenty of affixes (both prefixes and suffixes) occur in the second stage, especially if we treat such endings as **-s**, **-es**, **-ed** and **-ing** as suffixes, but in the third stage we find particularly the words formed with more than one affix (*affixation* itself has three) and the extended word-families that they fall into. This stage is under way for some children as early as the age of 9, for most by the age of 12, and will go on throughout secondary education if not beyond.

I have to repeat that this set of stages is much tidier and more distinct in my description than in practice. Even so, it provides a useful way of looking at children's errors. A child of 13 who is writing *culb for club, *jumb for *jam* and *shoos for *shoes* is showing phonic problems surviving from an early stage. One who is still writing *buton, *hamer and *writting has probably acquired those patterns rather later, and the writing of *dissapoint and *acomodate has been learned, or left uncorrected, much later still. The stages overlap a great deal, of course, but it is always perilous to assume that a polysyllabic word mis-spelled by a pupil under the age of 16 is a habitual error: the odds are that it is a first attempt.

**The first stage**  The process of learning to read (and therefore learning a large part of spelling) is concerned with three sets of relationships:
1   The correspondences between single consonant symbols, or letters, and the sounds they represent. Except for **c**, **s**, and to a lesser extent **g**, these are one-to-one.
2   The correspondences between the single vowel symbols and their sounds, where a given symbol may correspond to more than one sound, as with **a** in cat and hall.
3   The sound correspondences of the complex (two-symbol) vowel symbols, i.e. the vowel blends.

These spellings are in practice those found in the early stages of all reading schemes, based as they very properly are on one-syllable words of natural English origin and high frequency in the language. The problems for teachers of reading are of two kinds: the multiple correspondences of single vowels, which children have to acquire by matching their knowledge of spoken language to what they meet in their readers, and the vowel blends. The vowel blends are worth listing in systematic form. They fall into seven sets:
1   Simple vowels plus **-e** (*die, hoe, due*).
2   Simple vowels plus **-e** with the final consonant enclosed or included (*hate, site, dote, mute*).
3   Blends with **-a** (*meat, boat*).
4   Blends with **-i** (*pain, rein, coin*) and their **i/y** forms (*pay, they, boy*).
5   Blends with **-u** (*taut, lout*) and **u/w** forms (*dew, row*).
6   Doubling (**e** and **o** only, as in *deed, boot*).
7   **ui** and its word-final form **uy** (*build, buy*).

The change from **-i-** to **-y-** and that from **-u-** to **-w-** at the end of a word forms a spelling pattern that runs through the language. These digraphs are given in tabular form in Figure 4 (page 74), and contrast with some of those to be found in foreign borrowings (such as *dais, deity*, etc. which may be digraphs but tend not to be vowel blends). They dominate the spelling problems of early writing for many children, but they are worth establishing because it is with them that later learnings may become confused. Consonant blends cause much less trouble because very few of those without **h** are blends at all. Even so, there are several three-consonant clusters to cope with. Fortunately these usually involve a plural **-s** or start with **n** or **r**, the first consonant having a similar effect on all the clusters where it occurs. Where the problem arises it can be tackled by assembling as many examples as possible and asking the children concerned to put them into their main columns. Thus, *sports, calms, slings* are plurals; *ankle, sparkle, waddle, mantle* use an **-le** ending; *inch, winch, ranch* are a group on their own, and so on. But the patterns involved will almost certainly become recognizable in the next stage.

The problem of one vowel symbol having to do double duty and correspond to more than one sound is a headache at the initial literacy stage, but it has to be lived with until the children begin to derive help from the interlocking nature of the spelling system. There are awkward pairings to be cited at every turn: *pain* and *pane*, *rein* and *rain*, *due* and *dew*, and many more. The reverse is also true: quite dissimilar sounds have identical spellings, as in *said* and *maize*, *dead* and *bead* and many more. There are two things to remember before we find these curiosities totally frustrating. What we might at first think of as a merely arbitrary way of spelling one sound in two ways proves on further inquiry to have some reason to it. In technical language, the difference is contrastive. Thus, *pane* relates to *panel*, *pain* to *painful* and *painless*, the link of *said* and *say* is echoed in that of *paid* and *pay*. *Dead* relates to *death*, *rain* to *rainy* and *rainfall* and *raining* and *rained*. Most of these links are of meaning, and the spelling preserves the meaning-link in the teeth of a pronunciation difference, a pattern we shall meet again.

This web of linkages of meanings and spellings runs parallel to and interlocks with a similar web of contrasts, whereby words keep out of each other's way. Thus, the contrast between *pain* and *pane* recurs in *plain* and *plane*, *main* and *mane*, *wain* and *wane*, *red* avoids *read*, *die/died* avoids *dye/dyed*, and scores of other words do the same. These contrasts may look quite arbitrary to infants and their teachers, but in the wider patterning of the system they have a very important part, and learning them soundly at the start has immense pay-offs later on.

**The second stage**    The central process of spelling-learning in the first stage is one of matching the text of early reading material to knowledge of the language and vice-versa. It builds up a store of known connections and patterns which relates predominantly to one-syllable words. By the age of 7 most children are encountering two-syllable words, and only a few of them are familiar one-syllable words with such endings as **-es**, **-ed** and **-ing**. Many of the first stage words, however, will be forming families of themselves from these basic affixes, such as

     part   parting   parts   parted   partly   part's   party

and thousands of other examples. Very few children fail to grasp that these affixes can make such families out of many of the words they know. The child who writes ★walkd, ★comeing or ★likly has grasped this even if he is not yet sure of the way the affixes are attached. The attachment rules matter precisely because of the vocabulary they make available. There is scope for some rote-learning, but even more for the use of parallels and analogies and (of course) extensive reading. The problem areas are those of **-e** deletion (as in ★comeing) and consonant doubling. Let me illustrate an approach by dealing with the second of these.

Consonant doubling has two parts to it. One is that a consonant between the vowels of a two-syllable word will usually be single after a long vowel sound and double after a short one (cf *timer*, *hammer*). The other part is that when the addition of a suffix creates a consonant between the vowels of two syllables the same applies. This explanation of the pattern might help adult readers (and not all of them) but it is not much use to children, least of all when set up as a formal rule with three or more logical steps to it. They need an intuition, a feel, for a pattern which cannot be grasped by learning or applying a rule. It is far better to go systematically through some sets of examples:

| | | | |
|---|---|---|---|
| robber | redden | pussy | button |
| dibber | sadder | missing | matting |

and so for other doubled medial consonants

| | | | |
|---|---|---|---|
| rubbing | muddy | kissing | betting |
| rabbit | budding | bossy | hotter |

| | | | | |
|---|---|---|---|---|
| robing | maiden | making | losing | loving |
| tubing | rider | liking | noisy | leaving |
| caber | tidings | leakage | raisin | movable |
| cubit | Tudor | stoker | dosage | waver |

This approach will not handle the problems of *manor/manner* and some similar pairs with medial **-n-**, which have to be learned one by one.

Where teaching uses parallels and analogies, as it widely should, it is better to keep the contrasted sets apart: putting them side by side to learn as a set of contrasts does not seem to help children who have problems. In part this reflects the fact that some children have a more strongly visual learning style than others, so that while most children will register that the proper analogy for *dining-room* is *dine*, some will insist that it is *dinner*, and *dinning room will be an intractable error. For most, however, parallels and analogies are important not just for the spellings they teach, but because they provide strategies for self-correction and patterns that will reduce the children's reliance on the teacher or dictionary: they are part of teaching the catching of spelling. The debate about 'caught or taught' always was too simple: spelling is caught if children are taught how to catch it.

What has been said about the inadequacy of formal rules as a support in spelling applies even more strongly to other affixation patterns, notably **-e** deletion and **i/y** alternation. Good practice observes the principle already: infants encounter the plural forms of *story* and *worry*, the past tense forms of *cry* and *try* and *marry*, and many other instances of **-y** becoming **-ies** or **-ied**, as well as the dropping of **-e** when **-ing** is added. Infants do not receive formal instruction in the relevant rules: they are offered examples and shown how the patterns work. The same should apply for older children, with the difference that a given family of words can be lined up with other families that work in the same way:

| | | | | |
|---|---|---|---|---|
| marry | marries | married | marrying | marriage |
| carry | carries | carried | carrying | carriage |

These sets of parallels, or analogy sets, are a basic device in correcting mistakes, not least because they forestall mistakes based on false analogy with existing errors: the child who spells it *hateing is likely to spell *makeing, *takeing and much else until the pattern is corrected.

In this second stage, too, a number of other features of the system emerge, many without teachers or pupils realizing it. The system has numerous markers, many of them grammatical: thousands of vocabulary words are turned into adverbs by the addition of **-ly**, into plurals or into verbs or into adjectives by appropriate suffixes. But there are markers which serve other purposes. For example, two-letter words in English are almost always grammatical words rather than vocabulary ones. When a similar-sounding word is a vocabulary word it is given a marker in the spelling: *so/sow, be/bee, in/inn, to/two* and many others. One of these markers is to double the final letter, which appears again in making surnames out of common nouns, as in *Ladd, Benn, Penn, Carr* and many more. Another marker, more subtle, occurs in the contrast between words that begin with a 'soft' **th-** (such as *think, thin, theory*) and those that begin with a 'hard' **th-** (*though, those, them*): again, the hard **th-** marks a grammatical word. Many of these patterns enter into the skills of proficient readers without their knowing it, and the same should happen through the extensive reading of our pupils.

The suggestion that there is more pattern to our spelling than has often been recognized is not a claim that is all regular. But to make full use of the webs of analogy and contrast in the language can often make some baffling problems penetrable. One of the most awkward areas of all is the group of words in **-ough**:

| word | contrasts | analogies |
|---|---|---|
| through | threw | – |
| dough | doe | – |
| rough | ruff | enough, chough |
| cough | (coffin) | trough |
| borough | borrow, burrow | thorough |
| bough | bow | plough, drought |
| ought | sort, fort | sought, bought |

The existence of a contrast in every case means that the spelling has (in part) a function of keeping out of another word's way. The contrast in the case of *cough* is with *coughing*, which a majority of speakers say exactly as they say *coffin*. Moreover most of the words belong in word families of their own which consolidate their shapes.

The second stage evolves slowly into the third, without a boundary to mark them off, and the spellings that classes have to learn cannot be separated into second stage and third stage ones, even if they are drawn from the errors in the pupils' written work. Neither the system nor any of its stages can be mastered at once or completely. There will be errors recognizable as having arrived a long way back, and it will help all concerned if infants are asked to learn the spellings of a small set of words they will want to use in their writing but which come from later stages. These include *any, many, once, aunt, laugh, minute, quiet, beautiful*, and a few pairs like *man/men, woman/women*; but each school needs to make its own list.

**The third stage**   From somewhere between the age of 9 and 13 onwards for as long as schooling lasts, the learning of spelling has to focus on how words are made up, on what the jargon calls affixation. Thus, *fix* can become *fixate*, *fixation* and *affixation* in turn. Moreover these and the other affixes available can combine with thousands of stems like *fix*. The linkages in the system at this stage can thus operate in two directions: outwards from a common stem into many combinations, and up and down into different stems using the same patterns of combination. Thus, *import-report-export-comport-disport* illustrates the one, while *impose-reside-comprise-disproportion* shows the other.

Many affixes involve spelling patterns arising in the second stage. Such errors will continue to need correction, whether they be of **-e** deletion as in *fixateing or **i/y** alternation as in *statelyness. The same holds for joining problems like *dissapear and *proffesor, but the third stage has to concern itself directly with the syllabic basis of affixation in order to forestall or correct such habits as *diffrent or *authoritive. The affixation system in English, and the language's habit of protecting spellings which reflect meaning–linkages, give us features that this stage can exploit in the teaching. Let us look at two examples.

One of the commonest types of spelling mistake occurs in *grammer, *definate, *differant, *emagrant, *medisine. These words belong to a large category of words whose common feature can be seen readily in gramm**A**tical, defin**I**tion, differ**E**ntial, m**I**grant, medi**C**al. There is in every case a related or derived form from where the pronunciation and stress gives us a clue to the doubtful spelling. (The problem often is to get pupils to see they are doubtful, as we know.) To use this pattern needs a grasp of the stem–plus–affix structure of English words. Some children acquire this grasp from their reading, drawing the (to us) obvious conclusions about how word-families hang together by structure and spelling. But many will not perceive it unaided, and classwork needs to develop this awareness. It matters not only as a resource to make the children more self-reliant in spelling, but also as a beginning to the work on the intricacy and later the resonances of English words.

The interlocking of spelling patterns, word families, and meaning links recurs in a way which neatly illustrates how our spelling is both phonic *and* visual. In several word families a spelling is preserved in the face of a sound-change to ensure that the family connection and hence the meaning–linkage is preserved and seen. These may be vowels, as in res**I**de/resident, def**I**ne/definite, palace/pal**A**tial, or consonants, as prodigal/prodi**G**y or resident/residen**T**ial. In some cases the change is there but we are not always conscious of it, as in fact/fac**T**ual or grade/gra**D**ual: English pronounces the **d** in gradual as a **j**, although most of us suppose we are speaking a **d**, and the same holds for reduce and produce (but not reduction or production).

It is in this third stage of the system that the case for recognizing the role of syllabic structure becomes clear. The painless way to establish this recognition in pupils' minds is for it to start in the way words are spelled aloud by teachers (and soon afterwards by pupils). It seems unhelpful to spell words aloud on a basis of two-at-a-time or in random groupings when the syllables provide a potential mnemonic and a later guide to word-attack. Thus, it is better to say H-U-N-T/I-N-G/D-O-N than H-U/N-T-I/N-G-D-O-N. If you are in doubt about the syllable boundary between two syllables separated by a single consonant, the rule-of-thumb should be to break after that consonant rather than before it (thus CON-SON-ANT rather than CON-SO-NANT).

The use of analogy, especially for corrective purposes, needs to avoid including false analogies. An analogy-set consists of words which not only spell alike and sound alike but share the same sound-to-symbol correspondence. For example, *service/justice/malice/avarice* form an analogy set, but *entice* and *advice* belong to a different one alongside *vice* and *splice*, while *basis* does not belong in either set. Textbooks sometimes break this principle: widely used examples juxtapose *vague* with *argue*, *weapon* with *disease*, where the real analogy for *vague* is *plague* and the analogy for *weapon* is *threat* or *sweat*. Some textbooks actually invite children to obtrude a **d** in *privilege* by setting it alongside *hedge*! There are plenty of analogy sets available without using false ones, and they can be traced from each element of a group of complex words. An example of an analogy map of this kind is given in Figure 5 (page 74) but there are other ways of laying it out on a blackboard.

## Diagnosing and treating error

I have already suggested that the stages of acquisition in spelling provides a useful basis for identifying the nature of errors. Most spelling mistakes occur in comparative isolation: only a minority of children make an error in every other word, but it is with that minority that it is very useful to know which mistakes to leave alone and which to tackle. The general pattern of tackling phonic defects first, consonant doubling next, **-e** deletion and **i/y** changes later still, should be helpful in such cases. At the same time, it is not necessary to be sunk in gloom if a new class exhibits a very poor level of spelling. Until a class has registered that its teacher is not tolerant of careless spelling, at least a third and possibly half its errors will be mere slips. The simplest way to deal with them is to have pupils sift them out, their own first then their neighbour's, before work is handed in. Beyond this one needs a routine. Thus, many good teachers establish with their classes that while they will usually underline a spelling mistake, to write the correct spelling in the margin means writing it out three times, unless there are five such entries, in which case they have to be followed up, but it can be remarkably effective in impressing on a class that spelling matters. The other impression a class needs to have, of course, is that spelling can be learned. Confidence in their ability to learn is crucial for success in learning in all fields, and most adults attach such a disproportionate weight to minor spelling errors that children easily pick up a wrong sense of proportion. So the worse a class performs in spelling in its writing work, the more important it is to build their confidence in what they know before going on to deal with what they so far do not know. This means spelling tests chosen from words they have written correctly, at first. Ten out of ten all round the room does wonders for a demoralized class.

It is perfectly proper to ask children to learn spellings for homework, and usually helps with parental support as well. The method of testing is worth a little thought: the test can set the words with different endings or prefixes, or enclose them in a dictation, or ask the children to write a short story that uses them all. The checking, however, cannot be done merely by reading out the right spellings: too many children are visual rather than oral readers for it to be wise to omit writing them up.

The best spelling work, based in the desire to foster self-confident use of parallel and dictionary, reinforced by a rich reading programme, nevertheless has to face a problem that becomes increasingly awkward in the 12–14 phase: in many choices between alternative spellings these approaches and strategies do not help us. Guard or gaurd? Advertise or advertize? Inheritence or inheritance? Dispensible or dispensable? Writing it down to see if it 'looks right' is drawing on our accumulated visual imprint of the system where our morpho-phonemic knowledge ceases to help. Analogy can sometimes come to the rescue if we use it flexibly: *guard* parallels *guilt*, *guide* and *guarantee* – once again there are more analogies available than we realize until we stop to look for them. The determination to be correct at all costs, however, can lead pupils and teachers alike into quite unnecessary anxiety. The dictionaries allow alternative forms surprisingly often: forms in **–ise** and **–ize**, some forms in **–ance/–ence** exemplify what is known in the jargon as free variation, where either spelling is correct. The pressure to be always correct may also mislead children into thinking that no self-respecting adult ever makes a spelling mistake.

## The disputes about spelling

Two widely known disputes have raged over this topic. The better known is the long agitation for spelling reform, which is usually conducted in an understandable but extensive ignorance about language and speech. The gap between the sounds we actually make and the sounds we think we make is wider than we might suppose. The teacher who asks her pupils to correct *peculier by asking them to listen to how it is said is missing just this point, because what almost all of us say involves a final unstressed vowel of no clear quality at all. So, too, the parent who objects to schools encouraging 'lazy speech' is apt to overlook the absence of any **t** sound in her own regular use of 'don't'. But there is also a gap between what we suppose letters stand for and what we actually use them for. Thus, the **g** in *sign* is part of the vowel symbol **ig** that occurs also in *malign*, and both words have family connections in *signal* and *malignant*. This is the flaw in Shaw's famous argument. He made great fun of how the English really ought to spell *fish* as *ghoti – gh as in *enough*, **o** as in *women* and **ti** as in *nation*. But the argument works both ways: to be as consistent as that would force us either into an alphabet of over 40 letters or into spelling *judge* as *juj or *dgeudge, and the cure would be worse than the disease. The bigger problem with spelling reform, though, is to make the patient take the medicine: converting Great Britain to driving on the right would be simplicity itself in comparison. In any case, considerations of 'lazy speech', or spelling reform, or other adult notions about language are a digression from the main business of the learning that happens between 9 and 14.

A more important debate has involved remedial specialists in particular but affects all English teachers. This is the question whether the spelling system should be viewed as mainly acquired visually or mainly acquired orally. The debate is not merely misleading: it does damage. Teachers who emphasize the visual dimension neglect the oral one and vice-versa. Pupils for whom the oral dimension has been neglected will reveal the fact in such habitual errors as *probly, *scintific, *authoritive, while those unattentive to the visual dimension will reveal it in *collum, *daisey, *descison and so on. In either case children have suffered because the kinds of attention they have been led to give to text have been incomplete, lacking the stiffening of systematic study of word-formation, word-families, and their extension into derived forms. Children also need to be equipped with strategies for self-checking, which include the visual check of 'Does this look right?', the 'intuitive' check of 'Does this feel right?', and the analogy check of 'Does this fit with its relatives?'

A third debate about spelling that has engaged some attention is the argument about whether it is best taught or 'caught'. As the title of this chapter suggests, I think this is a non-debate, which arose from attitudes to English teaching that so firmly rejected the arid methods of traditional grammar schools that they threw out all forms of instruction as well. The avoidance of teacher-instruction in many junior schools in favour of group work is a different matter, and as I have suggested elsewhere may do as much damage in its own way, but very few teachers nowadays cling to the notion that one does not need to do anything about spelling in classrooms of children between 9 and 14.

## Using dictionaries

It was wisely said that the value of a dictionary lies in how much its owner does not need to use it. This chapter has suggested four sources from which we acquire a mastery of spelling: example, pattern, analogy and authority. By comparison with any of these, the role of learning by rote can never be more than marginal: learning ten spellings every school day for five years would provide most children with secure grasp of no more than a twentieth of their use-vocabulary and with a vast amount of useless lexical lumber besides. Example and pattern do their instructive work best when the learner is least conscious of them, for example when the reader is absorbed in the plot of a novel or in reading on cue correctly in a play-reading. I have emphasized the role of patterning because of its prominent place in our spelling and the comparative ease with which children make sense of it. Analogy and authority need conscious action, which will have to be that of the teacher at first. The whole drift of what I have said about analogy is that children need to learn how to develop analogies for themselves. The same has to hold for the use of authority: it is not enough to put child and dictionary together and hope learning will happen. Children need to learn or be taught how to use dictionary and thesaurus alike, and a sound introduction to study skills (see p. 7 above) is desirable for the able and essential for the rest.

Children between 9 and 14 need two kinds of dictionary: the kind to carry round and the kind to look up in the classroom. A portable one needs above all to be light in weight without being illegibly small, and there are several published for schools (i.e. as non-net books) that come as cheap as any of the fist-sized tinies on sale in shops and far more useful. Far better would be the Oxford Intermediate or its competitors in the Collins and Chambers ranges, but teachers should not take it for granted that their pupils will have seen the 'How to use this book' page to be found in all of them. The classroom, every classroom, needs to be equipped with a dictionary of reference quality, meaning a volume running to forty thousand head-words or more. There are several to choose from, and there is very little need to concern ourselves with the academic debate about whether a dictionary sets out to prescribe, to give correct meanings (such as Oxford's *Concise*), or defines words as having the meanings they are given in the current usage of the language (such as the *New Collins Concise*). What does matter is that the entries should be reasonably easy for ordinary children to scan. In particular, the scope and detail of the abbreviations may not be the practical virtue the catalogues suggest, and the habit of giving meanings in a historical order with the oldest coming first (which is the guiding principle for the Oxford dictionaries) may be a source of difficulty to children unaccustomed to it. By these standards, the Chambers *Twentieth Century* and more than one of the Longman list are strong competition. Ideally there should be enough of these more solid dictionaries in a school to make it possible to bring half a dozen of them together for group work on 'advanced skills' now and then.

One of the staple activities of English work in thousands of primary and middle school classrooms is the collecting up of words, usually written on a board, for use in an impending piece of writing. Tracing the precise meanings is for the dictionary, but assembling the possible alternative words is for the thesaurus. The standard one, written by Roget in the mid-nineteenth century, is still in use, but schoolchildren need simpler ones. The most useful for 9–14s are Green's *The Word-Hunter's Companion* and Rowe's *The Word Finder* (both Blackwell), and in the classroom they complement each other neatly. For English teaching with children of 14 and over, a copy of Roget in the current Penguin edition is as desirable as a good dictionary for every classroom.

## Conclusion

Let me summarize the basis of good practice:
1   Take spelling seriously and convey to your pupils that you do so.
2   Remember that the quality of your pupils' reading will be a major determinant of their performance in spelling.
3   Use every device you can to build a self-confident belief that spelling can be mastered.

**4** Develop that habit of looking for patterns and analogies so that children can work out spellings for themselves rather than be always asking the teacher.

**5** Link this with the systematic use of dictionary and thesaurus as a check.

**6** Be discriminating in your treatment of pupils' errors, so that early errors in danger of becoming habitual are given priority over mistaken new words or mere slips.

**7** Establish a routine between yourself and the class about how you will treat mis-spellings and what you expect them to do in response to your various treatments.

**8** Avoid referring children to 'listen to how it is said' and ask them to 'see how this looks when written' instead.

**9** Remember that, unlike mathematical tables, almost all spelling rules are complicated in their wording, difficult to apply, and open to exceptions.

| | | | | | | | |
|---|---|---|---|---|---|---|---|
| **1** i o u | +e = | | ie | oe | ue | (*die, toe, due*) | |
| **2** a e i o u (+C*) | +e = a+e | e+e | i+e | o+e | u+e | (*hate, here, mice, mole, cute*) | |
| **3** e o | +a = | | ea | oa | | (*heat, goat*) | |
| **4** a e o | +i/y = ai/ay | ei/ey | | oi/oy | | (*rain/pay rein/key coin/toy*) | |
| **5** a e o | +u/w = au/aw | eu/ew | | ou/ow | | (*taut/law feud/hew lout/bow*) | |

*i.e. final consonant enclosed (technically, included) between the V and the -e.

*Figure 4   The vowels and vowel-blends of the 'basic' system of English spelling*

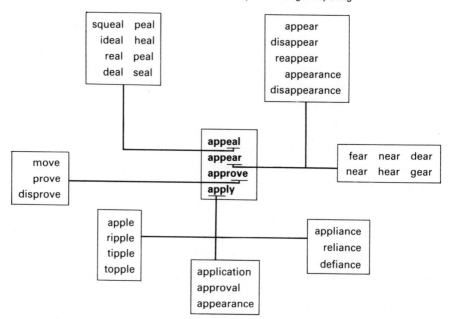

*Figure 5   An analogy map. Words in analogy sets spell alike, sound alike, and share the same sound to symbol correspondence.*

Chapter 7

# Writing good modern English

I have referred earlier to the need for children to learn not only how to write, but also how to distance their writing from the habits and patterns of the spoken English they learn first. The phrase 'good modern English' found so often in examination syllabuses really means, above all else, language in which that distancing from spoken styles is complete. That is, in spelling (which is a written-language affair by definition), in punctuation (which also does not occur in speech because it is a set of marks on paper), in the structuring of the discourse into sentences, and in matching the conventions of written language about sentence organization, managing complexity, tense, number and the whole area of qualified meanings – what Ogden Nash once called 'perhapsish-ness'. These elements in distancing our writing from speech are the substance of this chapter.

The logic of treating punctuation and sentencing in this way stems from the underlying principle that children will not learn to write 'good modern English' while they retain the unexamined notion that writing is speech put down on paper. Such topics and their treatment, however, take us into the territory of 'grammar', a word which means at least two different things which need different treatment in school. Everyone needs some general knowledge about words, and schools can justly be found wanting if pupils are ignorant (or even merely forgetful) of the parts of speech and a few other useful terms. But nobody should fall into the trap of supposing that knowing a few verbal labels or studying analytic rules will improve any child's ability to write very much. Grammatical rules are like spelling rules, so abstract as not to be much practical use. The property of grammaticality is very desirable in written English, but there have to be better ways of getting at it. I propose to explore both aspects of 'grammar', quite briefly, and to outline what teachers can and should be doing about them. At the same time, we should not be deluded by the notion of 'good modern English': acceptability matters far more than pedantry, Cabinet ministers seem inclined to routinely split infinitives, authors regularly find prepositions to end sentences with. And start them with 'and' or 'but'. So let us not strain at these gnats while swallowing our culture's far more questionable usages of language about such matters as race, or equality between the sexes, or other similar issues of human value.

## Graphic marmalade or essential scaffolding?

Some people are such skilled readers that they can obtain all the meaning in a written text without any attention to the punctuation whatever. Most readers of this book would be able to follow almost all of it if I left out all the punctuation. For others, however, the punctuation is a vital key to what they are reading. And perhaps once in 100 pages the presence or absence of a comma will radically affect the meaning. While the first kind of reader can tell at a glance where sentences or clauses end, the second kind needs the stops and commas to tell him. So punctuation endures as necessary scaffolding for some people all the time and most people occasionally. Its established status becomes more obvious when writers exploit it, by leaving it out as e e cummings did, or using it in overdrive as Henry James did. The conventional argument that punctuation matters because without it our meanings may be muddled or uncertain is rather a weak one, because examples of muddle or ambiguity are quite hard to find. The real argument is that sentences and their parts interact so closely with their proper punctuation as to make the latter an integral part of reading and writing skills. Almost invariably, the competent punctuator will be a better reader and a more fluent writer. Part of the meaning of 'competent' in this context is that the writer punctuates as he goes along: putting in the stops afterwards invites mistakes and impedes sentence construction.

## The punctuation system

English punctuation operates in three sub-systems: the marks proper, the inclusion markers, and the sentence-stops.

**The marks**   These include dash, hyphen, solidus (or /), italics, underlining, ampersand (or &), abbreviation mark, apostrophe and speech marks. Some of these reappear in pairs among the inclusion markers (see below). Apart from the apostrophe, each of these marks generally has only one meaning that can be looked up in a manual – the best is Collins' *Authors and Printers Dictionary* (Oxford). But the English are fertile with written language: once a device is invented and accepted it tends to acquire a second function. Thus, the full stop was borrowed for marking abbreviations, and the hyphen has several functions. It became common in facilitating a process of word formation that can be seen in such sequences as *post mark/post-mark/postmark*. This process takes a varying span of time but has speeded up as it has become more common (cf footballer, rainwater, rainguage, waterline etc. etc.). The hyphen then became the end-of-line marker for broken words, extended into usages such as *end-of-line, out-of-date* etc. (which are unlikely to coalesce into single words) and eventually developed a semi-quotation function, as in 'He called this a once-in-a-lifetime chance...'. These extensions of the hyphen's uses have made the prescriptions in many a textbook out-of-date, which is bound to happen with attempts to rigidify a changing thing like language. We can see the same process in reverse, too: it is conventional to advise the young to avoid dashes or ampersands or abbreviations in 'good modern English' (meaning formal prose writing), but all three can be found in abundance in the classical English novelists.

   Of all the marks the most awkward is the apostrophe. It is an unmitigated nuisance, serving to confuse more than to clarify, justifiable to children only on the most hollow formalistic grounds, and rapidly falling into disuse. Some textbooks still in use tell us there is an apostrophe for syllable omission as in '*plane* or '*bus*: the usage disappeared by 1950 or so. Textbooks also tend to juxtapose, and sometimes muddle up, the two uses that do remain, marking letter-omission (*I'm, don't, they've*) and possession. The tidy-minded have invented the myth that these two are really the same because the possessive case used to have an **-es** ending whose **-e-** is now replaced by the apostrophe. Sadly for the myth-makers (mythmakers?), most words now apostrophized came into the language long after possessive case endings went out of it. Less mythical but also inaccurate is the tenet that letter-omission is incorrect. If there is a custom, it is that where it denotes informality it is out of place in formal style, but good novelists have used it in less formal styles for two centuries. The apostrophe of letter-omission belongs in classwork at the age of 10 or 11, erroneous use of it earlier being tolerated.

The apostrophe of possession now suffers from overkill, as we see from its flowering in ordinary plurals on market stalls. Barrow-boy usage (as in *Tomatoe's 25p*) may engulf us all one day, but there is a clear logic about *Tom's 25p* and *Pot's 15p* with their marked letter-omission. I fully expect the apostrophe to have dropped out of newspaper and novel printing within twenty years, but to squeeze it out of school English is likely to take twice as long again. Until then, it would be wise for teachers to keep the possession marker separate from the marker of letter-omission, describing the former as 'shorthand for *of*' or even as '*of* built in', and teaching it by drip-feed from the age of 8 or 9 onwards without making a great solemnity out of it.

**Speech marks**   The best practice I have met discourages children from trying to use them at all until the third year of the junior school. There follows a set of stages, each lasting between two and five weeks, in which the work is interwoven with the routine English work and only in brief stretches absorbs it entirely. The stages go like this:
1   The children (in groups) read aloud scripted plays, one reader being assigned the stage directions where they extend to full sentences.
2   Using ideas developed in discussion and supplemented by the teacher, they work in ones and twos writing scripted short plays of their own and some of them are read through.
3   The children are asked to add to their plays, or write new ones, with no names of characters repeated every line unless there is a change to a new one. This drives most of them into the next stage quickly.
4   The part-names are replaced by say-phrases ('said' or a similar verb with speaker's name). Stage directions begin to drop out.
5   The children write a new dialogue, with the say-phrase varied, using a verb that acts as a stage direction to an actor reading the part – 'objected', 'wondered', 'exclaimed' and so on. At this stage the stage directions disappear.
6   The children are asked to look at conversation passages in novels and to make lists of the punctuation and layout features that appear there which they have or have not used themselves.

**7**   They are asked to write stories containing conversations, using as the only 'rule' the principle that speech marks enclose what-is-said-and-its-punctuation. The assessment is done with printed passages from novels alongside for comparison.

Teachers experienced in using this approach maintain that instruction in direct speech at an earlier stage makes life very difficult, and that it is wise to pursue the stages for at most half a year and then give it all a year's rest. Secondary schools, too, should avoid re-teaching it annually and should review their textbooks, many of which still assert traditional but quite erroneous rules about double inverted commas and other superfluous commas and capitals that have long since disappeared.

**Inclusion markers**   Here is a passage from O'Brien's *Mrs Frisby and the Rats of NIMH*, printed without its punctuation:

> although she was a widow her husband had died only the preceding summer Mrs Frisby was able through luck and hard work to keep her family there were four children happy and well fed january and february were the hardest months the sharp hard cold that began in december lasted until march and by february the beans and peas had been picked with help from the birds the asparagus roots were frozen into stone and the potatoes had been thawed and refrozen so many times they had acquired a slimy structure and a rancid taste

I have heard a hundred skilled adult readers try to read that passage aloud without preparation, and none has managed the first sentence: it looks at first as if it ends at *summer,* but in fact it goes on to *well fed.* That is, *her husband had died only the preceding summer* is an aside, an insert into the flow of the sentence. The same is true of *through luck and hard work* and *there were four children.* The alert reader may identify a fourth such phrase inserted into the flow: *with help from the birds.* These inserted phrases are not peculiar to this writer: there are four in the opening paragraph of this chapter, and ten pages opened at random in Jane Austen, Dickens and Lawrence reveal the same pattern with much the same frequency. It is so common that Quirk and his fellow grammarians gave it a label: inclusion.

The characteristic feature of inclusion emerges best when a passage is read aloud: most readers will alter their pitch slightly at the start of an inclusion, and at the end of it will return to the pitch-level they had before. The characteristic pitch-recovery associated with inclusion is apparent in all four instances in the extract from *Mrs Frisby,* although in varying degree. The commonest punctuation of an inclusion is a pair of commas, but O'Brien's original punctuation may be a surprise:

> Although she was a widow (her husband had died only the preceding summer), Mrs Frisby was able, through luck and hard work, to keep her family – there were four children – happy and well fed. January and February were the hardest months; the sharp,

hard cold that began in December lasted until March, and by
February the beans and peas had been picked over (with help from
the birds), the asparagus . . .

The paired dashes and the brackets are not in fact naughty Americanisms: there
is excellent literary authority for them in most of the major English novelists
and not a few of the major essayists. It is only modern purists who have
objected to them.

The point to note about inclusion markers is that they occur in pairs: the
comma that marks the start or the end of an inclusion can be submerged, as it
were, in a sentence marker, but otherwise both the commas are obligatory.
The absence of the second comma in such pairs is probably the most
widespread punctuational error among adults, and it reflects both an
incomplete sense of the link with speech and the absence from almost all
textbooks of any awareness of pitch variation in the way we speak and how we
use it to convey meanings. (Ask a class to work out a dozen different meanings
for 'Yes' or 'No' in speech, and then to try and write out in full what each one is
trying to convey.) Work-card material is easy to prepare on the model of my
extract from *Mrs Frisby*, for pairs of children to read aloud unseen, then read
aloud prepared, with pairs discussion of the punctuation. Before leaving
inclusion we might note, also, that quotations and titles can sometimes be used
in ways resembling inclusion (called 'apposition' in the grammar books), so
that quotation marks share with brackets the feature of always occurring in
pairs.

## The sentencing system

We have already seen that punctuation cannot happen in speech: it is a system
of marks on a page. In principle the same is true of sentences: they are a feature
of written language. They correspond to some of the features of speech, but
the correspondence is not an exact one. The basic unit of writing is the
sentence, but the basic unit of speech, the 'chunks' into which our discourse
falls quite naturally, may not always form a set of sentences. The 'tone group',
as the basic chunk of speech is known, can range from one to fifteen syllables,
and what proportion of a speaker's tone groups are also sentences depends on
his own style, what he is saying, who he is addressing, and so on. Tone groups
have their own patterns, which because tone groups are spoken are usually in
the 'tunes' or pitch contours. In ordinary statements, the pitch tends to drop at
the end. In questions it tends to rise at the end. (Does it? Read it aloud and see.
If you speak Geordie you will find this pattern is reversed, and other accents
have their own variations too.) So ordinary speech certainly uses sentences,
but is not bound by them, and its sentences are not always tidily arranged.
Writing down, therefore, may entail some rearranging and tidying up.
Writing that has not started life as speech is supposed, of course, to come out
already tidied up, but children are not always fully aware of what that means.

The most obvious way in which the tidiness required of written language may be missing is in the preservation of spoken forms. These are easily castigated as 'slang' or 'colloquial', but the process of learning to recognize the boundary between the 'usable in speech' and the 'permissible in writing' is a long and difficult one – partly because it is changing all the time, as a look at editions of the same newspaper only ten years apart will reveal. More seriously, however, this learning is difficult because some textbooks and teaching treat colloquialism as solely a matter of vocabulary. That is, we find plenty of attention to swear words and peer-group or in-group jargon, this concern shading off into less certain treatment of ethnic-minority vocabulary, and we find stress on the danger of transcriptions like 'wouldn't of', but these are relatively superficial aspects of spoken language in relation to the real demands of writing. The real concern needs to be with the ways in which written langauge allows sentences to organize meanings, where the contrasts between spoken and written can be far-reaching – so much so as to give some written styles the properties, for many children, of unfamiliar dialect.

The differences between spoken and written language in the way they organize meanings at sentence level are at least of five kinds. We have already mentioned one, the difference between tone group and sentence, where tone groups do not always have to have subject and verb. Mastering this requirement is part of the agenda of infant and lower junior writing. Second, written language can arrange itself in different order. Or, we might write, differences of word-order are available to written language. With more elaborate sentences this difference can be crucial – sentences can begin with an if-clause, a when-clause, and so on. To put it another way, we might write, 'If a sentence has a lot to say, and if the writer is trying to be careful about his precise meaning, and if he wants to say it as a single and coherent whole, he can write a sentence beginning (like this one) with three if-clauses.' But no-one would speak such a sentence: it would lose the listener before it got to the point. Thirdly, written language has to be explicit: it cannot afford the luxury of saying 'You know I was saying yesterday . . .', still less the use of implicit reference as in 'We was going round ours . . .': writing has to say who *we* are, where and what *ours* is (beside which the usage *we was* is trivial). Fourth, written text can refer to itself, set up and make use of links and threads all the way from my use of *second*, *third*, and *fourth* in this paragraph to the thematic imagery of darkness in *Macbeth*. The fifth is the existence of an almost hidden network of linkages that make each sentence bind or cohere with its neighbours to make a paragraph or a chapter. In this paragraph alone, for example, such links occur regularly: *organize meanings* (first sentence), *have mentioned* (second sentence), *this requirement* (third sentence) all refer explicitly to the preceding sentence in each case. Other examples of this network are *or*, *to put it another way*, *But*, *And*: once the search is on for such ties between sentences they are not hard to find. But teaching them like other formal properties of writing will be quite ineffective, and to describe them in any detail would take another book. (They occur naturally in writing by many children, too, as we saw on pp 47–48.)

Learning to write prose which is fluent without being tied to speech is a major educational achievement, and takes a very long time. In spite of the emphasis this book has placed on reading aloud, there are plenty of people who have mastered such writing without any marked skill in aloud-reading, and plenty of fluent aloud-readers turn out to write rather bad prose. The problem with learning to write is that formal instruction in definitions and concepts is of very little value. Thus, few children up to the age of 14 can grasp the concepts involved in such terms as 'subject' or 'predicate' or 'finite verb', but their writing needs to be able to operate with those features long before that age. The belief that children will write better prose if they know some grammatical rules is widely held but quite at variance with experience in schools. The ability to identify compound or complex sentences seems to have no spin-off in the ability to write them: like most textbook activities, such exercises presume the mastery of the skills they purport to teach. The real route to writing competence is more difficult: through sustained, absorbed reading of well written prose – prose, that is, which uses sentences in the ways we look for in our pupils' writing. The reading programme set out in Chapter 3 bears most directly on writing competence, although the bearing may take a long time to become apparent.

One way in which the linkage between reading experience and pupil writing can be facilitated will now be evident: punctuation does more than simply mediate between speech and writing, because it both allows us to represent speech features in writing and to structure written sentences independently of any link with speech. The basis of this remains, however, the way the punctuation system handles pitch, and this is a reason for being serious about reading aloud. The process of distancing written style from the habits of speech can be attacked more directly in class in several ways:

1   Ask a pair or small group to listen to a short tape of dialogue, and then to write it in the written conventions.

2   Take a prose dialogue from a novel and convert it, through written script with stage directions, into a radio tape.

3   Devise conversational exchanges in which each speaker says only one word, full of intonation-borne meanings, and then write the dialogue out with all the meanings made explicit.

4   Explore how some very long sentences should be handled in aloud-reading.


**The sentence stops**   The sentence stops are the comma, colon, semi-colon and full stop. The question mark and exclamation mark are variants of the full stop, which means that they are always followed by a capital letter. It is often said that the sentence stops form a scale from the lightest, the comma, to the heaviest, the full stop, but this is not strictly true because the colon has a special function distinct from the others.

*The colon* (:) has only one meaning in sentence usage: what follows it explains or elaborates what precedes it. (I have used one example in that sentence, and several others occur in this chapter.) In practice very few children up to the age of 14 ever need to know how to use the colon, but there is a case for ensuring that children from the age of 12 know its meaning for recognition purposes.

*The semi-colon* (;) is in reality rather different from a 'heavy comma'. I have already referred to the way sentences within a paragraph hang together in meaning and often have these connections marked by words like secondly, moreover, however, for example, even so, etc. In much the same way, writers often want to make units, which could quite well stand on their own (as sentences), hang together with other such units within the wider frame of the sentence. Here is an example:

> The most interesting Japanese posture is bowing, which is a form of greeting, like a handshake. Bowing is used to establish relative status – the less important person bows lower; the more important can establish his superiority by bowing less low than the other, or there can be a competition in politeness; in any case each watches the other carefully as he bows himself.
>
> M. Argyle Bodily Communication (p.90)

In practice the semi-colon is becoming rare. The steady trend of writing style in English is towards simpler structures in which the semi-colon is replaced by using separate sentences with the tie between them made explicit. The loss is hardly very serious, and there is now no need for formal instruction in the use of the semi-colon: students who want it can read up the manuals for themselves. This holds for the subsidiary use of it too, where a long list of items is organized into groups, each item being marked off by a comma, each group by a semi-colon.

*The comma* (,) has three separate uses. We have just met the use for marking off items in a list, sequence, series or collection (as in that example). We have also met the earlier case, using the comma, in pairs, to mark an inclusion. The third use of the comma occurs in the preceding paragraph, for example after *serious* and after *too* in the last sentence. This use marks the completion of a sub-unit of a sentence yet to be finished: it would be possible to round off the completed sub-unit with a full stop, but the comma signals that the sentence is going on. The stylistic convention is that it has to be followed by a connective of some sort, a conjunction or a relative. It is this use of the comma that traditional textbooks have associated with pauses, but what it really does is to allow the speaker/reader to acknowledge a new start being made within the frame of the sentence. In speech this would be marked much more often by a change of pitch than by a pause. In some cases the comma almost becomes a seeking of permission to re-start the sentence 'tune'. Hence, it occurs in sentences that go on too long for the speaker/reader to encompass in one go, even though the mere length involved is in no way objectionable. This comma too is often mishandled, usually by the loss of the ensuing connective:

> John's work in Geography is falling off, he needs to try harder.

A colon or semi-colon would serve here, too, but rarely does.

The listing comma and inclusion commas belong in the 'in passing' agenda: items to be built into routine comprehension discussion between teacher and pupils several times between 9 and 12, picked up when they occur in group or class reading. Confirmatory exercises may be worth while, but not of both at the same time. The structural comma is a more major teaching point: it needs to draw on example, and the aim needs to be to develop an intuitive feel in the student. By the age of 14, errors need correction and rules (e.g. 'Solo commas don't make connections unaided'). This brings us to the most intractable of all written-language defects, the run-on sentence. For example:

> After my breakfast I put on my walking shoes and went upstairs
> and got my satchel and came downstairs and put on my coat and I
> went out to meet my friend on the way to school . . .

One of two different things is going on here. Either the writer does not know how to structure serially narrated events, or he is importing into writing the sentence-final, attention-retaining 'and' of the club bore. To relate this to pitch, either there is a fall on *shoes, upstairs, satchel*, and so on; or there is a pause of some sort after *shoes'n, upstairs'n, satchel'n*, etc. Either way, there is a need for some one-to-one instruction, with examples of good writing practice. And in both cases, probably, the writing that is being asked of the pupil is more mature than his reading experience has equipped him for. The corrective work will succeed if the background exposure to written text is there; if it isn't, the correction is trivial in the absence of a stimulus to read and read and read.

## Teaching punctuation

To teach punctuation as devices taken out of context will increase the tendency for it to become graphic marmalade, spread on the dry toast of the pupil's writing after the event to keep teacher sweet. Far better to take a few pages of examples from a class's writing and set them out as sheets for small groups to work their way through before reviewing them on the board (or, best of all, the overhead projector). There is a case for asking a group or a class, too, to collect all the punctuation devices of a particular book and set them out as a system – say, at $9\frac{1}{2}$ and again two years later. Even that approach risks the confusion that stems from juxtaposing easily confused items, as in trying to teach *their/there/they're* as a set, instead of setting *there* alongside *where, here*, etc., and so for the others. But punctuation does not give us much option because so many of its symbols do double and even triple duty. Hence, each school needs its own policy and scheme, and needs to guard against the pious but usually vain hope that leaving it all to be taught 'in the context of the children's own writing' will lead to anything other than total neglect.

## Teaching grammar and being grammatical

The term 'grammar' has a technical meaning, referring to the descriptive analysis of language structures and usage. Such terms as aspect, inclusion, modality are part of its necessary technical vocabulary. 'Grammar' also has a commonsense or everyday meaning, which refers to our general knowledge about the parts of speech and other such features. Most people use the term, and its related form 'grammatical', in a third, normative sense, denoting beliefs about what constitutes correct usage. Most of the debate about teaching grammar in school arises because these three meanings become confused. The technical linguistics aspect does not need to belong in school English at all, even at sixth-form level. The general knowledge aspect has the same status as what happened to the wives of Henry VIII: useful general knowledge, but not something that advances our historical or linguistic insight or skills. The normative sense is the one laymen intend when they claim that schools should (or fail to) teach grammar. Challenged to give examples, such critics usually cite cases of colloquialism. Challenged to outline a syllabus, they lapse into incoherence. For their preconceptions have not grappled with the reality, namely that teaching children bits of grammatical information does not lead them into grammatical behaviour. This was demonstrated by research in most parts of the English-speaking world before 1960. However, no research can remove the perfectly reasonable demand that schoolchildren should know some of our basic grammatical terms.

There are some popular notions of grammar which are false. For example, a speech accent or dialect may be different from standard English, but that does not make it ungrammatical: there are forms of English where 'we was' is standard usage and 'we were' would be socially inept. Some would argue that all speakers of overseas dialects should adopt British English if they come to live here. This is tenable but linguistically unreal: children learn the speech of their community. Some argue that British English is 'contaminated' by its adoption of foreign words and phrases. Again, this is unreal: the foreign borrowings in this paragraph alone include *grammar, notion, false, example, accent, dialect, standard, usage, inept, argue* – removing such 'contaminations' would make the language unusable. There is no way of using the school system to impose a standardized speech form, and the record of efforts to use it to impose correctness of sentence structure is not encouraging. Children will write what they are motivated to write, and the teacher's task is to motivate her pupils not only to write, but to write acceptable prose – which means labour, example, and school-wide policy and coherence. So-called systematic instruction in sentence patterns has proved a will o' the wisp in several English-speaking countries.

## Labels grammar

It is reasonable to ask what items the 'linguistic general knowledge' of a pupil aged 14 should include. The great majority of primary schools have always taught the parts of speech, whatever the myth-makers claim. Many children have then borne out e e cummings nice observation that 'down they forgot as up they grew' and secondary English departments have not always insisted on refreshing their acquaintance. We thus have many adults who once knew about doing words and describers but admit to no knowledge of verbs and adjectives. The collapse of labels grammar in secondary school English happened in 1960, for reasons too complicated to go into here, and some of it is now being reinstated, not always with the happiest of textbooks. We also have large numbers of adults whose school knowledge of grammar goes back beyond the mid-60s and is likewise based on sources that were not always quite accurate. The complete list of items in labels grammar that need concern us is this:

the **lexical** parts of speech: *noun, adjective, adverb, verb*
the **grammatical** parts of speech: *pronoun, preposition, conjunction*
**gender** (*masculine, feminine*)
**number** (*singular, plural*)
**tense** (*past, present, future* only)
**auxiliary verbs**, **subject** and **object**, **active** and **passive**
**infinitive** and **participle**, **agreement**
**prefix** and **suffix**
**person** (*first, second, third*)

Of these, only the first five lines need concern children up to the age of 11, and possibly the last line. With older children as well as juniors, experience and experiment alike suggest that the standard course-book technique of drip-feeding one exercise a week causes confusion. It seems better to treat grammar like another topic or project, and go through the whole set (as far as is necessary) as a coherent sequence. Many teachers like to change the labels for other words like 'doing words', and there is nothing wrong with this. But the translating of these earlier labels into the technical terms cannot be left to chance: that is the failure of linkage that convinces most parents that schools don't teach grammar any more. (The system does not deserve that conviction, but its currency is the schools' fault.) This general position can be found well implemented in Michael Newby's witty set of textbooks *Making Language* (Oxford).

The besetting danger of a list of labels is the urge to elaborate. Take the case of verbs and their tenses, which in English are only two, present and past. All other verb forms in English are handled by auxiliaries: it is foreign languages that have future tenses, conditional tenses and so on. The key auxiliaries include *will, may, would, have, is, being, been, might, going to*, and it is worth noting that in spoken English the vast majority of futures are formed with *going to*, not the *will* or *shall* of the textbooks. (Textbooks in English as a foreign language, of course, know better.) For most other verb forms in English we find two other sub-systems of what the technical grammars call Aspect, which may be either perfective or progressive or both:

| Aspect: | | perfective | progressive | perfective-progressive |
|---|---|---|---|---|
| **tense** | | | | |
| present | he teaches | he has taught | he is teaching | he has been teaching |
| past | he taught | he had taught | he was teaching | he had been teaching |

To suggest that these variations are 'imperfect' or 'pluperfect' does not fit the grammatical facts as it does where an inflected verb has endings denoting tenses. Tense up to the age of 11, then, should confine itself to present and past; beyond that children can have fun putting together the auxiliaries and listening to how they are used in actual speech.

## Sentence types

A similar set of misapprehensions affects sentences, which are said in most textbooks to be of four types. The real position is not so simple, because English uses emphatic forms in alternation with unemphatic ones:

| Type | unemphatic | emphatic |
|---|---|---|
| **Statement** | Tom, lad, you left the door open. | That door's still open! |
| **Question** | Do you leave doors open at home too? | Is it still open, Tom? |
| **Command** | Would you close it, please. | Shut it! |
| **Exclamation** | – | What a wind! |

The exclamation almost always begins with a wh-form like *what*, and in its one-word form, unless it is a verb, is the interjection, a part of speech left out of the list earlier because it is in practice very rarely found. This account enables us to see that the exclamation mark would be more correctly called an emphasis mark.

Even so, there is more to sentence types than this. The original English school grammar of 1784 insisted, since all its rules were drawn from Latin, that every sentence had to have a finite verb. This does not fit the facts of English, which can be more accurately described by recognizing two broad categories of sentence, major and minor. The minor sentences puzzle children because they do not fit the traditional definition, but in every other respect they behave like ordinary sentences – convey a complete meaning, leave no part of the message out, secure an answer, and so on. For example:

| | |
|---|---|
| Sister: Is that you, Joe? | (Major, question) |
| Brother: No, Ken. | (Minor, statement) |
| Sister: Good day at school? | (Minor, question) |
| Brother: Could be worse. | (Major, statement) |
| Sister: Mine was terrific! | (Major, emphatic statement) |

In many spoken examples it can be hard to tell major from minor, and the common primary school rule requiring subject and verb is a quite proper search for major sentences as the written norm. At the same time, a total ban on minor sentences in narrative can make the writing of some children unnecessarily stiff.

## Concord or agreement

Many teachers alert to the oddities of language have heard a pupil take a text in standard English and read it aloud in their own dialect, using *we was* for 'we were' and *you was* for the standard written form, and have found on closer inquiry that the pupil is unconscious of making the change. This unconsciousness is revealing, because it shows how deep-seated are the dialect forms used in speech: such children will with luck grow up with the ability to write the standard form as easily as they speak the dialect one. The position with the majority of children is much less clear cut: children need an unusually strong attachment between their speech patterns and their social group if the influence of school is to have no effect on their speech. For children without this close attachment, which is to say for most, the problem of concord or agreement becomes the most obvious battleground between the two language influences. The battle acquires a destructive and probably unnecessary edge when teachers believe they can teach children to write correct English only by forcing them to correct their speech as well. This is almost certainly erroneous. What British English calls false concords (such as *they is*, *he be*, etc.) are quite likely to be the only normal concords in a speaker's natural dialect. It fudges a crucial issue to pretend that school can correct the natural speech: school can (and should) correct the learned written form, and the correction is helped by pointing up the contrast between written and spoken. The situation is one to be exploited, too: sympathetic exploration of the relationships between non-standard forms (which may or may not occur in written form) and standard English can be valuable classroom work on the social level as well as the linguistic, and should contribute to the wider approach to self-expression.

Such 'head-on' exploration of meanings and how to word them is necessary for another reason. We are familiar with children who avoid a word because they are unsure of its spelling. Sustained study of children's writing suggests that they avoid much more than words: they shy off novel or tentative ideas, especially speculative, 'perhapsish' ideas like the ones for which adults have *would* and *might* and *could have been* and *must have seemed* and many, many more. What these modal expressions (to use the technical term) have in common is perhaps a greater degree of contrast between how we say them and how we write them – and the modals are crucial instruments of precision in good writing. Much can be gained here by asking pupils to tape-record ordinary conversations or events, have them rehearsed orally in class or by playback, and setting brief extracts for different groups to transcribe – some groups doing a literal version, some transcribing into the convention of writing. This work is best done at 11 or 12, before adolescence makes the children self-conscious, and begins a marked change in their attitudes to language as a result.

Chapter 8

# Oral English

The conventional definition of the subject matter of English tells us (in, for example, the Bullock Report) that it consists of reading, writing, listening and speaking. To go from that definition to view the classroom activities of English as fitting firmly into one or other of these four activities is too simple and rigid. The account of reading in the first part of this book is a picture of activity that constantly spills over into listening to books and poems being read aloud, and into doing the reading oneself, into talk about poems and stories, and so on. The account of writing similarly treats listening and speaking as activities which naturally arise in the course of writing work. The purpose of this brief chapter is not to alter that emphasis, but to draw together the scattered threads about oral aspects of English.

Listening is a very difficult task if you don't want to do it: nothing is so easy as 'switching off' one's attention and thinking about next weekend's party or last week's lovely weather. One consequence of that is that children (and adults) will listen more attentively if their minds are on the subject matter being relayed than on the task of listening itself. Knowing one is going to be given marks for an activity raises the anxiety level at once, and for listening that kind of anxiety is particularly obstructive. In any case it is quite needless: there are plenty of fascinating things to listen to for their own sakes. Certainly children of 9 and 10 who have never listened to radio or tape have a skill to acquire but also many treasures to find. They and older children unfamiliar with all the variety of language need unfettered opportunity to learn how to distinguish some of its variations. These include differences of voice quality, and I have seen classes of third year juniors do remarkably acute work on the range of voices in *The Archers*. Work on voice quality spills over readily into accent, and the ability to listen attentively to a range of speech accent without prejudice is becoming a social necessity in a multi-cultural society which is easier to tackle at 9 than at any other age. There is room, too, for work which asks children to listen to a tape of speakers in a range of contexts and say, from what they hear, what is going on, and it is not hard to make such a tape from a single morning's broadcasting that will include a sermon, an interview, a news report, a radio lesson, and so on. Once made, such a tape can be used with several classes, of course.

Testing children for their 'listening skills' (whatever they are) is pointless, but that does not mean that the listening they are asked to do should lack focus. Children should come to take it for granted that if the teacher reads a short story there will be discussion. They should expect to be asked what they had been hearing in Assembly, should assume that a clutch of poems read aloud in class will lead to talk about them in twos or threes. Until the class have acquired these as routine expectations it will be necessary to signal them before the listening starts. Children and teachers also have some surprises in store if they have never included a tape-recorder among the listeners and compared recollection with event, and the same surprise awaits those unaware of how much more a second hearing of a tape can reveal than was heard the first time.

In any case, tell children (or adults) that their listeners are to be given marks for listening and they will start elocuting with gusto. 'Speaking' in the context of oral work refers much less to formal addresses than to discussion in twos, three or fours. Such talk is rule-governed: we all observe some 'rules' about conversational exchange, timing interruption, throwing the ball to another or having it thrown back to us, showing you want to speak. It would be surprising if children of 9 knew these habits – plenty of adults have still to acquire them – but between 9 and 14 some of them will begin to emerge, and in most classes there will be a handful of pupils who need direct instruction about them by the teacher in a small group. There may be a handful, too, at the other extreme, whose problem in discussion is not so much constant butting in but never saying anything at all. One of the teacher's tasks with a new class, then, is to assess its level of competence in discussion, in terms of the language but even more the social awareness it calls for, and to provide situations which will build on the competence displayed.

The starting-point has to be pairs-talk, in which children are asked to discuss a simple issue with one neighbour. The discussion needs the focus of a specific question: was the villain justly punished, or how did an event not explained in the story come about. It is usually wise to find out the answers or responses. Less easily answered questions follow later, where a show of hands will not yield an answer, but one member of the pair has to give some explanation of the pair's view, and monitoring the responses may involve eliciting four or five responses in this way. From pairs-talk the logical move is into groups of four, and shortly after such a pattern starts it is wise to ask each group to elect a leader who writes down the conclusions and reports them – a role that can be rotated once a month. When the groups change size and pattern in this way the tasks given to them will need to be made more specific for a time, until the social learning has adjusted to the new groupings. Whatever the size of groups and the nature of the task, however, sound work in discussion means ensuring that children know what they have to do. It is better to tell a class that they have 14 minutes for a task than to say 'Take the rest of the period for . . .'. It is better to say 'Leaders to bring me a note of three main comments about this poem' than to invite the class simply to discuss it. It is better to say 'You have ten minutes, and each group will be asked to tell the class one argument for and one argument against,' than to ask a class to get into groups and 'Discuss the pros and cons of . . .'. These structurings do not cramp discussion work by children: they release it by giving them something definite to work with.

There are many reasons for treating whole-class discussion with some caution until you know your class and they know you. The purposes of whole-class discussion are in any case different from small-group talk. Its best use is to bring out into the open the issues and feelings that children on their own will conceal or refuse to acknowledge, and because sensitivities are involved it is best focused initially on literature, especially poems. Even with a class the teacher knows very well there are dangers in using whole-class discussion for some issues without preliminary small-group work, and some literature can raise such issues clearly. There are several good children's novels and stories now available, for example, which deal squarely with 'Paki-bashing' and other odious features of British life, and this comes up for discussion in a whole class setting which includes some Pakistani children only if the teacher is very much in command. All this is saying that discussion work is not a substitute for other classroom activities that involve more obvious preparation. Many classes will demand to be allowed to 'have a debate', while being light years away from accepting the conventions of formal debate, and that is precisely the kind of request that should be refused. The labour of teaching them those conventions is scarcely worth while: those who want to debate will learn them from existing debating societies soon enough. But a class that comes in the day after a major political row and says, 'Can we have a debate about hanging?' (or corporal punishment or supergrasses or whatever the issue might be) is giving the teacher an invitation. It may very well be right to scrap the planned lesson and say 'Not a debate, but we can have discussion-in-fives, with topics.' The phrase 'with topics' refers to the simple but invaluable technique of writing a question for discussion on the board every ten minutes. The separate questions break down a large issue into manageable ones, and each group must of course produce a note of its answers to each one. There is abundant experience among specialist teachers that discussion work of this kind, taking place for a period every week over the whole school year, becomes with secondary pupils a very influential part of their language learning and in many cases has a most impressive spin-off on their handling argument in writing. Providing this opportunity at 14 and 15 entails letting the pupils acquire the necessary skills much earlier, and the work gives the teacher an insight into how her pupils think and feel that is available in no other way.

By comparison with discussion, the other speaking activities of the English classroom are much less important. The speaking skills do include that of being audible to a group without being too loud, and opportunity to acquire this ability arises in reading aloud, the use of scripted plays, telling the others about a good read, and so on. The only one of these activities not previously dealt with in this book is the use of scripted plays. This book does not attempt to deal with drama, whether in its improvisation form or as play production, but the use of scripted plays as classroom reading material falls outside both and has its uses. Scripted plays have been very much out of fashion among English specialists in recent years, partly because of the prestige of improvisation approaches, but chiefly because published plays have presented the familiar choice between difficult classics and rubbish, with very little in between. Nevertheless, there is a good case for finding one or two full-length plays to read in class in a school year as soon as the texts are within range of the interests and reading skills of the pupils. Here again the continuities are relevant: pupils of 15 need to be able to bring some oral play-reading skills to bear on dramatic literature and fiction. Thus, reading a play by, say, Shaw, which can happen in a great many classes aged 14–16, needs the skills of taking good note of the stage directions but not actually reading them out, of managing the timing of interruptions, rapid exchanges, dramatic surprise, and so on. Such skills need to extend, by the age of 14, to appreciating and making good dramatic use of the pointed diction of plays like *The Importance of Being Ernest*, the dramatic force of *Royal Hunt of the Sun*, or the psychological tensions of *Journey's End*. These strands in the literature read by middle-secondary classes also form part of the bridge to Shakespeare – to the verbal fencing in *Romeo and Juliet* or between Beatrice and Benedick in *Much Ado About Nothing*, to the pathos of *Richard II*, and the tensions and complexities in *King Lear*. To put this another way, Shakespeare will be out of reach of children at 14 *if* their previous experience of theatre excludes attending a live or serious play or studying the scripts on which live theatre rests. A large part of the problem of accessibility to Shakespeare lies in the lack of access to other kinds of plays from much earlier.

A first approach to the format of plays can use the *Take Part* books, designed mainly for infants and young juniors: stories are told in a play script format and the parts are written to be within range of specific but various levels of reading ability. Some of the books are suitable for older juniors, but they need to lead on into plays of a more adult character. The one-act tradition of trivial plays designed for amateur players does not bear on school work, but there are long and useful lists from several publishers, varying from conventional three act stage plays to television scripts of all kinds. They often provide children with a high point in an otherwise tedious routine of classes, which means they tend to 'go' very well, and that can conceal the need to give a little thought to the activity. Here are some of the ground rules:

1   As with a novel, work out before you start what points you expect to reach in each teaching period.

2   So far as possible, work out the casting beforehand rather than be seen to yield to or reject a forest of waving hands seeking parts.

3   If it is practicable, devote most or all the available periods to the play so that it is read through reasonably quickly: to 'do' the play once a week sacrifices most of its dramatic quality.

4   Find ways of enabling pupils who are not so obviously fluent and mature to take prominent parts – for example by allowing some to take a copy away overnight to prepare their parts.

5   With children under the age of 13, 'do it again' is a better way into perceiving the quality of a scene than 'let's discuss it'. If you want to explore that nature of a dramatic surprise, having read the scene once, pose the question 'How is this surprise built up: *why* is it a surprise?' and ask a different cast to read it a second time.

6   Better still, such repeats with a necessary minimum of furniture at the

front of the room can give young readers a far greater addition of understanding and insight than adults might find credible.

Two illustrations of this last point are worth giving. A reasonably able class aged 13 had begun exploring Shakespeare by looking at particular scenes – the play by the 'rude mechanicals' in *A Midsummer Night's Dream*, the verbal battle between Petruchio and Katherine in *The Taming of the Shrew*, the murder scene in *Julius Caesar*, and the deposition scene in *Richard II*. A visiting theatre in education group came to the school, and asked it to suggest some scenes it might include. They had *Richard II* in their repertoire, and after the scene's performance one boy asked about the bitter lines

> Though some of you with Pilate wash your hands,
> Showing an outward pity, yet you Pilates
> Have here delivered me to my sour cross,
> And water cannot wash away your sin.

Had it been deliberate, asked the boy, that during the long formal speech of abdication, Richard had stood there with his arms out in the position of a cross. The actor nodded and returned a question: 'And do you know where he gets the washing of hands from?' – a question that sent class and teacher back to hunt through the text all over again for the hints of the deposed king as a martyr like the Christ, and one boy brought in a gramophone record of a first-class company whose performance gave this imagery its peculiar resonance.

Another example concerns Terence Rattigan's *The Winslow Boy*, which for obvious reasons figures in many school stock cupboards. It is about a naval cadet wrongly dismissed from the officer cadet school at Osborne in about 1904 and his family's determination to clear his name. The play does not make clear an aspect that will have to be explained to contemporary children: that a middle-class boy of that era would never be able to get a 'respectable' job in life if he had been proved dishonest. Within that only mildly artificial assumption the play is clear, strongly written, and contains at least two splendid scenes. In one of them a distinguished and formidable lawyer questions the boy aggressively before deciding whether to take the case. The whole drift of his questioning suggests that he takes the boy's guilt for granted, but at the very end he turns round and announces that he will take the case: 'The boy is obviously innocent.' It is not difficult to depute four or five pupils, one of them in the role of producer, to organize a second reading of the scene with the necessary furniture on some kind of stage (in a classroom or a drama studio, but not a full-size school hall), following the appropriate moves and actions. It does not matter how good their performance is: subsequent discussion of it in the class will bring attention again and again to the text and what it means. Children are not bored by the repetition: the interest lies in what their mates will make of it, and they can be very acute about how to improve a treatment. The boring thing is endless questioning by the teacher about texts whose language is, in the absence of performance, beyond them.

## Oral skills

Small-group discussion and the management of plays are only part of the oral component of English, and they have received emphasis here because they form the part that can most usefully be dealt with between 9 and 14, and have a bearing on aspects of the subject later on. The oral skills that matter for adult life are wider: making oral contact with strangers, responding at interviews, seeking and giving information and, especially, explanations. By comparison with that demand on oral competence, the kind of work done in schools under the guise of CSE Oral English is sadly inadequate. The examiners generally seek response in conversation with an unfamiliar adult, or with the teacher in the presence of an observer. There may be other activities such as reading aloud or giving a little lecture, but they are equally artificial and unreliable. The reason for this position is that teachers and examiners have mistaken product for process: they have looked for the content of what is said rather than the way in which the speaker communicates with his audience (whoever that is). A great deal more is now known about assessing oral competence than was available to those who set up the CSE oral tests nearly 20 years ago, and there is reason to expect considerable changes before very long.

The development of oral work in secondary English is likely to change over the next few years. Discussion with an adult, the lecturette and similar 'performance' type items are likely to give way to new approaches. Since the development of CSE instituted these methods, a great deal has been learned about simulations and how to make them into settings for purposeful oral activity. Another strand goes back to the work of a Schools Council project which issued some materials called *Concept 7–9* (E. J. Arnold) in the early 1970s. One of its key ideas was to set children in pairs with a screen between them, give each of the pair some material that differed in some minor way, and ask them to solve a problem without looking at each other's material. For example, Child A has a set of six pictures of varieties of bird or animals or vehicles, while B has only two of them, and A by question and answer has to identify which two these are. It is an upward extension of the familiar Logiblocs of the infant school. Again, Child A has a picture (of, let us say, an orange circle the size of a sixpence one inch above the top right hand corner of a pale blue two-inch square) and B has to draw the picture as accurately as possible from A's description: A learns most from the successively improved efforts B shows him over the screen. Just as searching is the task in which both children have maps, and A has to guide B to an unknown destination. This may seem close to the 'Now, Pat, tell the class what you saw when the test tube was heated' and many similar tasks that happen in many secondary subjects, but telling the class is quite difficult and to learn by first telling one's friend behind the screen can make a great deal of difference.

The underlying principle is to restrict a speaker's audience, prescribe the context slowly, create an interaction, and focus on content rather than success in the role of speaker. It is exactly this pattern that has been adopted by the Assessment of Performance Unit's Oracy Testing Programme that began in

1981. The Programme uses experienced teachers as assessors, and trains them in the work, most of which lies in observing how children handle the tasks. Thus, Child A with pictures of six seagulls has to establish which two of them Child B has, and so with pictures of box-girder steel bridges, or beetles or sailing ships. More searchingly, A is given a map for a walk from X to Y, but there is a new motorway blocking the route; B has an up-to-date map and has to direct A – but both are unaware that the intended route will take A in what will feel like the wrong direction. Assessors measure the performance of both. A final sample from the range of tasks in the APU programme asks two pupils to discuss, in a time limit of 30 minutes, how they would discover, by scientific experiment, which of four environments woodlice prefer, namely dark and dry, dark and damp, light and dry, light and damp. They are given a list of the equipment they would have, and both pupils are assessed on the quality of their discussion using criteria agreed for all assessments and applied consistently through the training of assessors.

The use of this approach to oral English by the APU should not lead us into supposing that it is solely, or even mainly, a testing device. The educational world is heavily laden with programmes and course schemes that advocate such principles: most of the best work in primary science poses the question, suggests where to look for the evidence, and leaves the pupils to work out how to investigate. The same principle underlies the teaching approaches of many middle schools in almost all subjects. Yet the prospect of diverting some of our English time to setting up such oral activities in order to develop oral competence may fill many teachers with anxiety: how shall we find room for the extensive reading, the poems, the drama, the imaginative writing, the spelling and so forth – a question to be addressed in the next chapter. And if we do all these other things properly will there be any time left for oral English? That question is as likely as not uttered in hope rather than anxiety, and this is not the place to propose for non-specialists an approach to oral work that very few specialists have begun to understand or practice. The development that I have described as in prospect will filter through the system gradually, and my account of it is meant to make it more recognizable when it comes – and to alert teachers to the scope for good oral extension work that exists in the everyday routines of English. For example, in assigning the role of producer among a group sent off to rehearse a scene, do you give it to the talkative bossy-boots or to the quiet girl who is quite well able to handle it but needs only the confidence of being given the job?

Chapter 9

# Putting it into practice

This chapter deals with the down-to-earth matters of organizing the work in the classroom, the balance between possible elements in an English syllabus, how to know whether learning is really happening, how to deal with assessment. Most of the teachers addressed in this book will have existing traditions and school habits to fit into, but some will look for help in adjusting to change, and any reader is entitled to know how I would expect to see my outline of English work implemented.

## Classroom organization

Most of this book's suggestions for good practice can fit the arrangement of desks in serried ranks facing the teacher, where the whole class does much the same work at much the same time, and the control exercised by the teacher is collective. The use of pairs and small groups for preparatory discussion of an activity is easily accommodated since most such arrangements allow for desks or tables in pairs with a second pair in front or behind to make a four. However, much of the English work proposed in these pages points to or would be more fully realized in a classroom where pupils were organized in three or four working groups which they adopted for most or all of their time. Between the formal fore-and-aft classroom and full group organization is a compromise now quite common in secondary schools, where the desks are rearranged to create a central well or a set of three or four focal areas. This may have to be negotiated with the caretaker or the cleaners or other users of the classroom. The merit of such schemes is that they provide a less forced grouping for discussion, comparing texts, and collaborative reading. They are not often as successful as groupings in primary classrooms which superficially look very similar, for the reason that successful group work entails much more than changing the furniture: the work the groups are to do needs changing too. At worst, grouping the furniture without planning the pupils' work fairly carefully leads to a climate of chatter and limited effort that quite outweighs whatever benefit the change may have sought in the first place.

The heart of what I am calling group organization lies in asking the groups to do, not their own versions of a common task, but different work which is tailored to each group's particular needs. This is not proposing the high idealism of individualized learning for all: that needs unusual resourcing, plenty of teaching experience, and usually rather more mature pupils than most of those between 9 and 14. It is open to the primary school teacher to organize her groups so they are pursuing different subjects at the same time, but that is not part of the scope of this chapter. The case for some degree of

group organization rests on some fairly obvious principles:
1   Pupils vary quite widely, even within a nominally streamed class, and group work permits a closer match between abilities and tasks set.
2   Group work places responsibility on children for their own learning, which increases self-motivation and exploits natural curiosity, so that the kind of control needed from the teacher changes towards a more co-operative atmosphere.
3   Group work relies on careful planning of each group's tasks and time, so that there is much less waiting about, use of time is better, and children always know what to be doing when they feel they have finished.
4   The same planning governs the teacher's deployment of her own time, ensuring appropriately varied kinds of attention to the full range of pupils.

The approach outlined here is assuming that grouping for English will usually be by ability, partly because the need to cater appropriately for varied abilities cannot be met fully in any other way, partly because this pattern is the most obvious next step away from a predominant weakness of most secondary English teaching today, the treating of mixed ability classes as if they were homogeneous.

Most teachers who have contemplated group methods, or have tried them and given them up, have found one or both of two difficulties to be insoluble. One is that the teacher has a marked adjustment to make in the way her own effort is distributed. One might over-simplify a little and say that the whole-class teacher puts an hour into planning the work for a six-period day and comes away with three hours' marking if she is lucky, while the group-methods teacher puts at least three hours into preparing materials and has an hour's marking afterwards – but the first never escapes the marking treadmill while the second can hope to use the long labour of preparation to build up her own bank of materials for use in future years. The other difficulty is one which looks much more of a problem to the secondary teacher than it ever turns out to be in practice: will not the children take advantage of it and cause chaos?

Children have two main needs in relation to classroom activity: to know what to expect and to know what is expected of them. Given a clear brief about how the work is to be organized, and shown that the teacher can and will set out what they are to do, with whom, for what span of time, with what outcome, children will normally welcome group work. For one thing, most of them have long experience of it. For another, being lectured at is no more successful a learning posture for children than it is for adults. At the same time, group organization has its besetting vices just as the traditional classroom does: what the lecture notes prepared two decades ago and never since revised can be to the latter, the quickly reached-for worksheet is to the former; the teacher who talks too much to the silently assenting class is not better than the teacher in a group-planned room who is pinned down at her desk by a queue of children waiting to have work marked. Moreover the adoption of group methods can be gradual and selective: many successful subject teachers use whole-class methods at one level and group methods at another, and a probationary teacher is well advised to have no more group-organized classes than her preparation of material can cater for.

## Two examples

Figures 6 and 7 (pages 106 and 107) set out in grid form the kind of planning and plotting that first class group organization calls for. In both of them there is a detailed timetable for who does what. Each group is an established one, the pupils all know what is expected of them, and the 'plot' is posted in the classroom for all to see. The materials for use in each segment would in real life be references to particular sources – textbooks and so on – which the children would know how to find if they were not already set out. And perhaps most important of all, the disposition of the teacher's own time is planned in the same degree of detail. The grids make the pattern seem more rigid than it would be in practice, but the children follow the timing without bells or announcements.

The first example occurred in the June of the children's second year in a junior school in a suburban part of a small country town. There are 32 boys and girls, three of whom need an hour's special help each week with reading. The class works in four groups for English and four (but different) groups for Maths/Science, usually with English first. Every Wednesday the English work is devoted to writing stories and poems, usually in response to a stimulus from a taped broadcast. On the other days each of the four groups takes one of four activity blocks in turn. There is not much variation in ability in the class, and the noise-level is very low, in spite of a good deal of purposive talk going on. On most days the group tasks begin immediately after registration, i.e. at 9.00 a.m. (the assembly is at a different time each day), but this is a Monday so the work for the week needs explaining. What the grid does not explain is that the particular materials and tasks assigned in three of the four activity blocks can be varied to match the attainment of the group.

Figure 7 sets out a rather different example. A 9–13 middle school which was once almost 300 strong has shrunk to just one form of entry, and the urban area it serves has become the focus for a large ethnic minority community, mainly Pakistani. The school's third year class, aged about 12, has 29 on roll, but two of them are very recent arrivals and spend their English time with the peripatetic language specialist or with the head. (There are four others nominally on roll, but they have been away in Pakistan for several months, and when they return will have to rejoin a younger class.) The remaining 27 children fall into three quite sharply defined groups. Eight children, not all native-speakers, have built up substantial reading experience and are between competent and able. They work well as a group, particularly for assembly presentations and devising ambitious science inquiries. They were advanced enough last year to have suffered very little from the marked bias of their teacher in favour of Maths/Science. The other two groups, in the judgement of their present teacher, show clear signs of that regime. Group 2 consists of children of average ability whose handwriting, spelling and interest in reading have scarcely developed beyond the level to be expected of 9 year olds, and even their Science writing is slapdash. The third group includes eight children, five of them resident in this country only for two years or so and deceptively fluent in spoken English but very restricted in their writing and easily led away from sustained reading even at a quite modest level.

Where the underlying purpose of group work in the first example is to create a climate for a great deal of oral interaction between the children on sometimes demanding questions, in the second case the purposes are to provide separately for a group that would be held back by the others in whole-class work and to enable the teacher to concentrate closely on the special needs of the other two groups.

These displays are greatly over-simplified, selecting out the formal activities and their time-planning, putting down in two dimensions a complex set of related processes happening in three dimensions and over a span of time. The effect of the description is bound to include an impression that the teacher has to be in two places at once, and certainly the teachers in both classes are on the move all the time, engaged with children all the time (one-to-one or in a group of at most nine), but there is no feeling, given or taken, of undue bustle or divided mind.

## One thing versus another

The next question to face concerns balance within the syllabus: what should be the relative weight of the various elements I have written about? Against the background of a subject as inter-related and constantly crossing over from one part to another, any answer to that question is going to over-simplify. So let me take a typical situation and make a model of it – not as an example for everyone to copy, but as a sample way of working out the sums. If the basics of the model differ in your own case, make the model afresh with your own basics.

The typical pattern in most junior and middle schools, and in a majority of secondary schools, is to apportion approximately four hours of school time for English. Many junior, most middle, and almost all secondary schools set this time out in segments or periods ranging from 25 to 80 minutes, with a concentration on about 40 minutes. I shall use the six weekly periods of 40 minutes as the basis of my model, and will suppose that from the age of 10 or 11 an odd half-hour or two is available for homework if needed. But English is not a linear subject which progresses from Item A in Period 1 to Item P in Period 16. In practice, good English teaching operates on the span of the term or the half-term. A term of 12 weeks will usually lose a few periods for half-terms, school functions and the like, so let us suppose we have 69 periods to play with. It will be easier to give the elements of English a weighting in periods per term (p.p.t.) than in minutes per week –

so long as we are clear that the aim is not a time-plot but a rough idea of orders of magnitude.

The p.p.t figures for each element would look something like this:

| | |
|---|---|
| Individualized silent reading | 12 |
| Original writing | 12 |
| Handwriting | 6 (i.e. 5 mins/day, 4 days/week) |
| Phonics/Spelling/word-formation | 6 (e.g. 5 mins/day, 4 days/week) |
| Language study (punctuation etc.) | 6 |
| Poems with discussion | 6+ ⎤ filled out with time under |
| Plays and drama | 6+ ⎬ Reading Skills but |
| Class reader/novel | 9+ ⎦ inclusive of writing arising. |
| Reading Skills | 3 |
| Other | 3 |

No sane English teacher cuts the work up in this way, but she does need the check that her allocation of time is reasonably in balance. We can put the order of magnitude of the elements of English in other ways:

1 If you combine the total class reading of poems, novels, plays etc. you should reach a total larger than that for individualized reading or original writing, but not much larger.

2 If you left out the handwriting, spelling, and language study you would save relatively little time in the short run – and might cost yourself a great deal later on. But if you left out either the class reading or the individualized reading you would be doing much more damage.

3 The weighting between the elements may well need to change between 9 and 14, but the way each of the elements is realized will need to change much more than its time allocation.

4 The weighting may sometimes need adjusting, perhaps quite radically: find out what you can about balance in the work the class did the previous year. If its work was thrown off centre by lax control or over-rigid use of bad textbooks, adjust the weighting and the class content as seems fit.

When we do have a clear sense of balance, what would it mean in practice? How much can we reasonably expect children of a given age to write in a given time? How much would they read? There is no way of giving a clear answer to those questions: if I were to pitch them where I might wish, many readers would throw up their hands in disbelief; if I were to be credible to the general run of teachers I could well seem undemanding to others. In any case, what is 'a page' or 'two pages'? But some basic requirements are obvious from the way in which varieties of schools and pupils respond to published materials:

1 Prose passages for reading with a view to discussion or some kind of comprehension activity for children aged 11 need to be of such scope as will allow development of ideas or narration: one cannot look for inference in a text with no implications. Such passages will have this scope at a length of 400 words or so, but much denser writing will do so

at half that length and more diffuse writing only at more. This matches the more subjective need for a 'real' fell to the reading, since most textbooks run about 300–350 words to the page.

2   On the writing side, children aged 12–13 need to be achieving work which organizes ideas or descriptions or narrative into five or more main blocks, preferably disposed as paragraphs, and each of them involving several sentences. If the scale of the paragraphs is of the order of 40–100 words (according to writing ability *and* the demands of the task) the scope of the writing demand will be extending the pupil's response.

3   Candidates for public examinations at 16+ will be expected by most GCE Ordinary Level examiners to have no difficulty reading a passage of 1,200 words or more, sometimes of considerable density, while the scale looked for in the written essay will be related (according to content) to a norm of 500 and 600 words. The ablest pupils at 14 will come quite close to these norms, and many others will do so shortly. The demand in CSE essay papers is much more modest.

But quantity, either of reading or of writing, taken on its own, is as poor a guide as quality on its own. In any case each teacher has to accommodate to and build on the habits and assumptions of the department she works with or the school as a whole. The state of the book stock, the pupils' level of attainment, what they did last year, and their attitudes to the subject may add up to a more constricting set of limitations than any departmental policy or syllabus. How far do the compromises that inevitably result need to be modified according to the age and abilities of the pupils? Where should adaptations occur? The individualized reading that I have described as indispensable ought to be habit already; if 9 year olds are not used to it, they will need to learn how to concentrate for 20 minutes at a time, and extending this to 40 minutes may take much of the year. With writing work the problem may differ, in that many 9 year olds may be unused to writing in silence, but they soon accept the discipline and find that they need more than 20 minutes to write what they wish. By the age of 11, however, many pupils find their teachers want to push the writing work into the homework time in order to liberate class time for other things. My view is that this is mistaken: it encourages some children to obtain their compositions from parents and allows others to evade writing altogether by exploiting the teacher's reluctance to confront. A very able class aged 13 or 14 might be an exception to this.

At this point some readers will look for a set of syllabuses, a series of linear specifications of what to do, period by period or week by week over the years. For me to provide that would be to repeat the error of many textbook makers and invite you to be used by my programme rather than to use its principles. It would be possible to compromise and set out one or two samples of typical weeks of English work at various stages, but as the samples given already will have shown, such slices of real practice are so embedded in their contexts as to offer relatively little help – contexts including the pupils, their attitudes and experience, the teacher and her knowledge, experience and nerve: one might almost offer as a rule the proposition that good practice in English teaching is identifiable by being original, by not being second-hand, so that even a lesson based on a well-known textbook passage is handled in a slightly new way, even the most hackneyed of schoolroom poems is treated or illuminated afresh. It is in the fractional innovation, the insistence of each teacher on being herself, that the nerve is required and the real quality lies. Prescriptions cannot give you that, and cannot in any case protect you from the occasional failure: even the most experienced English teachers have lessons that go awry.

## Progression

How do you tell whether the children are really learning? One part of the answer is set out in my chapter on writing development, where the indications of progression can be observed when they happen even if their occurrence cannot be engineered by the teacher. There are many other signs to watch for.

1   Motivation is so important to success in reading and writing that the attitudes of a class are evidence in themselves. A co-operative class that obviously enjoys its varied English work is more than likely to be making substantial progress in it. Most under-achieving pupils, moreover, respond to firm expectations more, not less co-operatively.

2   Find a comparable class and discuss its output with its teacher, making comparisons with that of your own, not in terms of personal quirks and habits but in terms of style and presentation and scope; look at handwriting, spelling, range of vocabulary and image, variety of sentence pattern, imaginative drive.

3   Pay a great deal of attention to the individual records of each pupil – whose job it is to maintain them in good, dated order – and observe the choices of reading matter. You may not find much change over two months, but over eight months or a year, apart from occasional regressions, you should expect a perceptible rise in the maturity and reading level of the books the children choose to read.

4   Handwriting and visual presentation should, if not improve, at the least not deteriorate: a falling-off here tends to signify low morale, and good work in English tends on the whole to look good – so much so that poor stuff well presented can win itself better marks than it should.

5   The clearest sign of all that children are progressing is probably their response to writing tasks. Children who begin the year with reserve often open out, become less wary of revealing personal feeling or private experience, and the level of trust within the class grows perceptibly. (This means being sensitive about reading a pupil's work to the class: some may assent to it while in reality hating and fearing the experience.)

The most false indicators of progress in English are the strings of marks for tests and course-book exercises. Formal examination results are also uncertain guides. The only published reading tests that reveal anything useful about performance in English are the *Edinburgh Reading Tests* (Hodder), which are expensive to buy and time-consuming to use.

## Assessment

More young teachers of English have been overwhelmed by the burden of marking than by any other problem. So it is worth pausing to ask what marks are for and why we mark pupils' work at all. The Cockcroft Report on Mathematics teaching observed that the 'sums' that most teachers spend time ticking and crossing are only a fraction of real Mathematics. Marks are a shorthand, a message system between teacher and pupil, which itself educates pupils about the kind of feedback to expect from teachers. Because marks are usually numbers they can be detached from their context, where alone their feedback function is valid, and treated as independent judgements, added up into form orders, awarded prizes and the rest of it. In English the use of numerical marks is particularly at odds with good practice: sound English teaching does not mark: it assesses.

This means, in particular, three distinct elements. First, the teacher is clear in her mind what is being evaluated and relates the form of the evaluation to it: marks out of ten will fit a spelling test quite well and nobody is the worse for using them. Second, the feedback function has quite separate, albeit related, roles as comparison and as support or stimulus. The children need to know whether they are being assessed competitively against one another or individually, each against previous performance, and if they do know they will interpret the feedback messages accordingly: the last thing to expect of children is that they can be fooled by teacher's marks. Thirdly, however much the school may press for marking to be competitive, in English it is important, so far as possible, to make it supportive and stimulative. That is to say, the pupil is open to strong influences when a teacher is returning written work, and the written comments added at the end of a piece of writing are usually valued very highly. Most children have so much of their self-esteem at risk in reading what a teacher has said about their best efforts that it is important to be positive if you can. The occasional burst of enthusiasm will do more good than most teachers realize, but the essential in these comments is to show that you have really read the text. If your comment refers to one of the characters by name, or to one of the main incidents in the narrative, that is itself praise: you have done the writer the priceless honour of paying the writing serious attention. By the same token, if you have to be critical, you may have to reserve that for face-to-face discussion, when there is time to pick up the good as well as the less good, when the resources of speech can blunt the severities of brief written comments. The best annotative comments from teachers are not afraid to express opinions, ready to reveal the reader's reactions, and apt to be full of suggestions about what to attempt next time.

How much the comments from the teacher can be judgemental and critical depends on the relationship between teacher and pupils. It also depends, of course, on how much time the teacher can spare for writing them. No English teacher can hope to give a responsive comment of much substance to a full class more than once a month, or to more than a quarter of the class each time it does a major writing task. Even so, the gains to be won from even this modest improvement on marks out of ten every time are well worth the effort.

### What if I can't spell either?

Finally, there are English teachers, not all of them specialists in other subjects, who have as much difficulty with spelling and writing as some of their pupils. There are teachers who would dearly like to take some English who feel debarred by weaknesses in their own spelling. What are we to think about such problems? Let me illustrate what I have said earlier about the potential of literature to illuminate our mundane as well as our more grave concerns.

Charles Dickens' novel *Our Mutual Friend* is a towering work about the horrors and hypocrisies of a London he knew very well, where wealth was grounded in the processing of waste, where every job-title or place-name might be a euphemism for the intolerable, where 'dust' meant sewage, 'character' meant bigotry and 'friendly' meant promiscuous. At one point in the novel we meet Boffin, self-made, outwardly self-important, a man of some wealth and no cultivation, who upon retirement looks to some self-improvement. So he finds and drags in off the street where he sells ballad sheets a little man with tiny spectacles and a wooden leg named Silas Wegg, whose sole claim on Boffin's attention is that he has read some of his ballads to his customers: he can read! In furtherance of his self-improvement Boffin has bought a well-bound set of Gibbon's *Decline and Fall* on a market stall, and he negotiates with Wegg for the latter to come in at five pence the hour to read it to him. So Wegg takes Boffin through the Roman emperors at a gallop, reading a text he manifestly does not understand to a listener whose hope of comprehension is even smaller. The scene is a resonant symbol of education in 19th century England. Teachers were to remain as educationally one-legged as Silas Wegg for a long time, and some of their masters remain even now as limited, arrogant, mercenary and philistine as Boffin.

Nevertheless, we enjoy a literate culture, which emerged from one where literacy was the privilege of a tiny minority. That emergence would not have happened if every person who had some slight anxiety about spelling had for that sole reason held back from the enterprise.

### Record keeping

There is a substantial literature on record keeping in primary and middle schools, including the work of a Schools Council Project and many sections and chapters in books on primary school practice. The problem with all of this well-meant advice is that it relates to records in the sense of documents passed on with the pupil, records in an institutional sense, but not to the needs of the individual teacher. If you are a Classicist taking on some English, or a junior teacher with Maths main, your own specialism does not provide you with any basis for knowing what to record in English work or how to record it. The principles to observe, however, are straightforward:

103

**1** Using a conventional mark-book, allow at least two double pages for each class for each term, and start the class list ten places down the page. This gives you a 'box' at the head of each column to note some detail of the kind of work sought and given, and enough space down each column to allow annotations alongside or in lieu of your numerical marks.

**2** Insist on a three-weekly check on the Individual Reading Record for each pupil, with occasional discussion of book choices.

**3** At least once in the spring term, and preferably at the end of each term, when you read each pupil's most recent piece of writing, make some conscious comparisons with the earliest work that pupil did for you and make a written note of what you find.

**4** In recording the marks for classroom tests, it may be useful to put different categories down in separate colours – blue for spelling, red for good work, green for language exercises, and so on.

The purpose of these habits is to put yourself in a position to observe both the improvements and the deteriorations, either of which may have a bearing on your teaching decisions and plans, on a broader basis than the selective workings of memory or the profound impression made by a simple piece of writing. The nub of it is that we tend to forget things if we do not write them down, and if we write down only some parts of the pattern we shall mislead ourselves about the whole.

## Display

There is a great deal of cant talked about display, as if any posting up of pupils' writing was better than none. Last year's art work and the time chart made by the first year class three years ago are not convincing additions to the visual education of this year's pupils, but the same holds for a tatty Sunday Times poster about *Othello* held up by a single drawing pin. English does present a display problem, all the same: its classrooms tend to offer no display or too much, suggesting that specialist English teachers need some guidance from colleagues about mounting, margins and spacing out. There must surely be a better way of using display than papering a whole wall, from waist level to seven feet, with dubiously legible pupil writing. Let me summarize the choices:

**1** Display must be used to convey approval, to disseminate, or to inform. Decide on the purpose and select material and method accordingly.

**2** Display for information requires high standards of visual presentation, and it is necessary to be fairly critical in selecting published posters, some of which, especially in the field of comprehensive surveys and time-charts, try to pack in far too much. Colour-supplement visuals from the 'heavy' Sunday papers are often very useful, but lose their impact after a week or so.

**3** Informational display of good quality will convey effectively facts and ideas that few teachers can handle confidently. How book printing handles page-layout and mechanical folding is a case in point; others include the technology of book-binding, how computer typesetting is done, the nature of 'electronic mail', how a newspaper makes up a front page, and the treatment of photographs in the media that is so brilliantly described by Harold Evans' *Pictures on a Page*.

**4**   Display of pupils' written work to convey approval is the terminus of a process that many teachers find useful, because the display is used to create an editorial imperative: 'Correct this and write it out in best so we can put it up. . .'. The incentive value is much reduced, however, if the teacher's wish to be 'fair' leads her to mount work from every pupil. It would be wiser to reserve the use of display for approval for work which commands such approval in relation to the writer's capacity, and if it needs editorial tidying up let that be done jointly between author and (usually) more proficient classmate.

**5**   Is it wise to display work with mis-spellings or poor handwriting even if they are the best that some pupils can do? No: either we mean business about these disciplines, or we don't. Posting up poor work undermines our own insistence that it is not good enough.

**6**   Display for dissemination is a different matter – display for such occasions as parents' evenings, open-days and the like. Here the need is not only to create a physical setting in which passing visitors will be led to stop and actually read, but to give them some help in knowing what they are reading. Classrooms wallpapered with writings are a classic switch-off for visiting parents. Schools do far better to arrange the room as a set of reading bases, equip each base with four or five ring-binders of material, and provide some very quiet background music. Each ring-binder has the output of a particular class, with an account of what context or stimulus led to it set out on the front. Once the parents know what to do with it, such rooms are often full, the backwash effect on the children is almost always potent, and the material can go all the way from remedial work to Advanced Level, educating many parents at the same time.

| | Block A | Block B | Block C | Block D |
|---|---|---|---|---|
| 0900 | Teacher describes pattern and content of the week's work to class. Review of last week's introductory work on synonyms. Introduce idea of thesaurus, distribute available copies to look at. O.H.P. showing how a word-finder or thesaurus is organized. | | | |
| 0910 | | | | |
| 0920 | Extended cloze-type exercise for work in pairs on synonyms (asking not for one answer-word but for a list of possibles in each space). | Group teaching about skim-reading – need, aims, method, samples, discussion, leading to | Handwriting drill (5 m.). | Handwriting drill (5 m.). |
| 0930 | | | Worksheet tasks about alphabetical order. | Group-reader tasks: 1 read story carefully 2 list main events 3 work out the ideas underneath the events 4 list the key details 5 write 2, 3, 4 down. |
| 0940 | | pairs – exercise requiring skim-reading of a text (which chapter for x?). | Group moves to the Reading Corner: changes of library books and long silent read of own choices. | |
| 0950 | | | | |
| 1000 | | | | |
| 1010 | Shorter individual exercise using same idea. | Individual skim-reading exercise on a text of next week's history topic. | | Group teaching: questions and discussion on story just read, building on ideas of skimming and what is missed if reader skims in wrong places. |
| 1020 | | | | |
| 1030 | Handwriting drill (5 m.). | | | |

Weekly pattern: Groups rotate daily, M. T.
Th. F. Weds: class story/poetry writing.

| | |
|---|---|
| Blue group | Blocks A B C D |
| Red group | Blocks B C D A |
| Green group | Blocks C D A B |
| White group | Blocks D A B C |

Notes
Shaded area denotes teacher's availability to pupils.
Block A: Reading Extension: last week Synonyms 1, next week Antonyms.
B: Reading Development: last week Using Contents Page and Chapter headings, next week skimming paragraphs.
C: Book-related work. Green group will have more teacher-support. Alphabetical order to second letter (next week, to third letter).
D: Focus of group-reader work varies with nature of the reader and the main class-work theme for the week.
Handwriting drills follow the Nelson scheme. Exercises, worksheets etc. may be self-made cards or extracts from textbooks or a mix of both.

Figure 6   *Scheme for group work from a sample week with 32 boys and girls aged 8½–9.*

| Time | Blue Group | Red Group | Green Group |
|---|---|---|---|
| 0930 | Teacher starts group off on a list of poems with a theme.* | Handwriting drill. | Handwriting drill. |
| 0940 | Each pair selects poem for joint reading aloud to class and rehearses. | Completing pairs-editing and fair copies of last period's writing ('Family Row' and other such titles); discussion allowed for 8 minutes then silence. | Reading with teacher – cloze and sequencing materials** to develop participation in discussing meanings and skills in reading for meaning. |
| 1010 | Different pairs set out to write poems/stories on the same principle or idea for teacher to see. | | |
| 1020 | | Teacher visits group twice in the 8 minutes and twice later, marking some work each time. | Sets periodic reading tasks while teacher attends to Red Group. Set written sequencing exercise. |
| 1030 | Reading of four chosen poems to rest of class. | Listening to the poems. | Listening to the poems. |
| 1045 | Discussion in response to teacher's question, 'Why those poems?' | | |

Notes
Shaded areas denotes teacher's availability to pupils.
*The theme of the work for the half-term is Relations Talking: the poems are thus to be conversation pieces and about families or relatives. The sources provided for the group include *Junior Voices*, *Voices*, *Poems 1* and *Poems 2* (ed. Harrison & Stuart-Clark, Oxford), and a number of the sources referred to in Morris – *Where's That Poem* (Blackwell).
**The materials are drawn from wide-ranging sources, mostly published textbooks, including Seely – *Reading with Understanding* Vol. 1 (Oxford).
Last week: Blue Group studied difference between scripted play dialogue and direct speech, writing samples of both; Red Group read up and planned for major piece of writing; Green Group concentrated on self-chosen novels for individualized reading.

*Figure 7   Scheme for group work from a sample week with 27 boys and girls aged about 12.*

## Chapter 10

# Some problem areas

This chapter deals with a small set of topics that relate closely to English teaching but are not central to it. Some of them relate closely enough for the specialist or the head of department to need to know about them, but for the ordinary non-specialist or novice struggling to keep a grip on the essentials they are subsidiary. Those who are devotees of microcomputing, or are committed to children with special needs, or to English as a second language may bridle at being so unceremoniously relegated to the second division of priorities, but there are many aspects of English teaching which are, quite properly, in the second division of *their* priorities. In any case they need have no fear: my purpose is to improve rather than hinder their dialogue with less specialized colleagues.

The case with drama is rather different: it is hardly a problem area, but this is perhaps the place to explain its omission from the book. It has its specialists and enthusiasts, too, who do not speak with one voice by any means. More seriously, the position of drama in schools defies generalization. In some it is a separate subject with a head of department and a suite of rooms; some treat it as merged with English; some treat it as no more than one of the peripheral skills welcome in an English specialist but not really essential; and some pretend it is not there. In addition, however, the practice of drama as a classroom exploration of feeling and its expression is peculiarly difficult to acquire from a book, and impossible to grasp adequately from the single chapter that this book would at most be able to spare for it. Rather than attempt the impossible I have left it out altogether. That should not be taken to imply reservations about dramatic methods or simulations in the hands of competent practitioners – on the contrary. It does imply reservations about the value of secondary drama work led by teachers without sufficient training to sustain it at fourth and fifth year level, where its educational potential seems to me greatly undervalued by many schools. For teachers in junior schools even a relatively limited training, if the trainer is expert, can open up quite unexpected dimensions, but this will happen the more readily and effectively with teachers who have overcome their initial classroom difficulties and anxieties.

### English and the microprocessor

This book is being written during the first phase of the Department of Industry programme for equipping all primary schools with a modest computer, at a time when almost all secondary schools have several but very few of them have diffused them among other subject departments. Moreover the typical schools micro has a memory of very modest capactiy, up to 32k in the jargon. Programs are usually loaded from cassette and printers are relatively rare.

These conditions can only be described, from the point of view of serious work in English, as primitive. Let me explain why.

At almost every point this book is trying to show the complexity of the continuous processes of language learning. Children enlarge their competence in language by extending their skills in reading, listening, speaking and writing. The extensions have to take account of the way these four modes interact (as in the multiple correspondences between sound and symbol in spelling), but also of the marked differences between them (as in the much greater speeds of thinking and reading than those of talking or writing). The learning has to take account, too, of the contexts in which all use of language occurs, contexts that are always linguistic and almost always social as well. Any computer program that purports to offer learning experiences to children needs to do likewise. It is not difficult, for example, to make a computer provide the materials for cloze procedure, or multiple-choice answers, or simple sequencing, or story prediction. But it is impossible to make it do so with a memory of only 32k like that of the Acorn B now found in many primary schools. And if the child using the micro is to have any serious benefit from the composing work done on the screen, there needs to be a printer to enable him to take the result away with him. The drift of all these considerations is towards the conclusion that serious work in English must wait until the next phase when hardware has developed a little more – when, for example, the longer programs needed for it can be stored on disk and loaded with reasonable speed. That generation of hardware is unlikely to be an economic purchase for schools for several years. In the meantime, sadly, programmers are bending their energies to design programs for the present generation of hardware, and in the nature of the case the results cannot be much more than trivial.

The immediate effect of the limited memory capacity of current micros is to make programs in language focus on specific features which relate to words rather than sentences and to sentences (simple ones at that) rather than paragraphs. The features of words that invite attention in this sphere, of course, are spellings. My chapter on spelling indicates some principles which are rather different from the traditional reliance on spelling 'rules', based on the proposition that our so-called 'rules' in spelling have so many exceptions and are so complicated to use that they cannot really be called rules at all. Even so, programs designed to teach the spelling 'rules' may have their corrective uses, but as a strategy for young children acquiring their grasp of the spelling system they do not take us very far. They also need to be technically accurate. To take a quite simple example, does a program dealing with 'Magic e' confine itself to the dummy vowel usage (as in *hate*, *rote*) and the dummy consonant (after v, n, z as in *love*, *gone*, *sneeze*)? Does it include 'lexical e' that identifies words like *house* and *lease* as vocabulary words? If it points attention to pairs like *rip/ripe*, does it also have to use pairs outside the child's range like *grip/gripe*? Does the programmer understand how i and y can alternate, so that these pairs can include *tip/type*, *hip/hype*, or does he think such pairs unsuitable because of the changed vowel? Teachers generally would exclude them, too, but would be unwise, as Margaret Donaldson suggests:

> The truth is that for most open letters – and for certain letter-groups – there exists a set of options in the sound system. The correspondence is not one-to-one, it is one-to-*n* – that is, one-to-two, or -three or more. . . It seems to be widely believed that children must not be told the truth about the system to begin with because they could not cope with such complexities. I believe this to be quite mistaken. What underlies the mistake is, I think, a failure to make a crucial distinction – a failure to see the difference between understanding the nature of the system and mastering all the individual patterns of relationship. It will inevitably take a child some time to learn all the sets of correspondences. The question is simply whether he will do this better if he is correctly informed about the kind of thing to expect. . . There is no reason to suppose that children of five cannot understand a system that contains options.

*Children's Minds* (pp 104–5)

In general it is much wiser to let traditional materials and methods undertake the setting of language-learning tasks where the focus is on the language items themselves. The best programs available at the time of writing for work which generates language-learning are in fields where most teachers would regard the language aspect as very incidental. To which my reaction would be 'Yes, precisely'. For it is when the learner is least conscious that he is developing new language strategies that he is most apt to be doing so. The pupil absorbed in a task, especially in a sustained and credible-seeming simulation, will use sentence structures new to his speech style quite unselfconsciously. Perhaps the best current example of computer-based simulations of this kind is *Saqqara* (Ginn): a beautifully detailed archaeological dig in an Egyptian pyramid. The children have to reach decisions about where to dig, how to interpret their finds, record every step, keep a full written diary, discuss each move – all the best features of topic work. In less elaborate activities, too, the computer may have its virtues: when the program is a game and the players have to issue the computer with two-word instructions, they have to get the grammar and lexicon of two-word sentences right. If the computer comes up with its near-despair line 'I must be stupid but I don't understand what you mean', the players have to talk out some very precise language to make any progress.

## Children with special needs

There are technical distinctions between such phrases as 'with special needs', 'with learning difficulties', 'slow learning', and others. I am not concerned with these fine distinctions, and at risk of offending the purists will refer to slow learners. But, and it can sometimes be a big 'but', a good many children learn some things slowly, while only relatively few children learn everything slowly. It is not only the 1981 Education Act, and the Warnock Report lying behind it, that have caused the national change we are now witnessing in the treatment of children with learning difficulties large or small, permanent or transient. The development of LEA curriculum policies, the weight of HMI reports, and the steady pressure of informed professional and parental opinion are causing closer attention at all levels. A major effect is to make the tradition that divides pupils between ordinary classes and the remedial department seem antiquated. It is being displaced by the realization that there are too many children who encounter difficulty at some time or another, and too few who encounter it all the time, to justify that way of organizing things. The need is being recognized increasingly for all teachers to know something of what to do for children in difficulty, without either jerking them out into the remedial department or leaving them to flounder. That growing recognition is yet to be converted into widespread practice or the skills it requires.

One of the reasons for slow progress in this sphere is plain panic: the prospect of having to teach slower learners or even handicapped children in ordinary classes fills many teachers with anxiety – about what to do, about how to recognize progress. The first of the answering messages to such panic is very simple: there is no mystery about the children and no mystique about teaching them. The need is not for new things to do, new techniques, but for different methods of doing the same things – especially different ways of wording their material and their tasks. The stress on individualized reading of whole books that characterizes my chapters on reading still applies, and the problem (to which there *are* solutions) is to find books which match the limited reading ability and greater age and less childish interests of such pupils. So, too, with the stress on bringing the written word to speech and the spoken word to writing, on group talk and activity on reading development tasks: these matter not less but more for the slower learner. It is a deeply destructive illusion to suppose that slower learners need exercises more than others, and a self-excusing complacency to argue that they (or any other children) benefit from inert exercises because they appear or claim to like them: they like boiled sweets, but. . .

For all children, competence at writing is in part a consequence of ability in reading, and reading performance is in turn governed in significant degree by ability in speaking. We first have to observe and assess the child's use of language. This is territory that Joan Tough has made her own, and she has shown that untutored commonsense is not enough: it is needful to know what to look for and how to record the changes that occur. Her main book for teachers is *Talk for Teaching and Learning*, and here is a key passage:

> We can be deceived about children's skills of using language unless we are able to analyse children's talk as we listen to them and discover what their limitations are. Making appraisals adds this knowledge to the teacher's resources. The following is a summary of characteristics of using language that put children at disadvantage in school and may only be identified as the teacher makes appraisals of each child's use of language:

1   The child may seem reluctant to talk or resentful of the teacher's questions. He may give short answers, shrugging off the teacher's approaches.

2   Some children may be embarrassed by talking with the teacher and look away, avoiding eye contact. Talking to the child when he is pursuing some routine task gives him legitimate reasons for looking away.

3   Children who talk readily may seem to ignore questions and instead initiate talk relating to present or personal experiences.

4   The child may rely heavily on gesture and on implicit reference, for example using 'thing' instead of naming.

5   The child may seem to lack adequate vocabulary but his real difficulty may be unfamiliarity with expressing ideas and with the need to make meanings explicit.

6   The child often gives a tangential response; that is, one which may have some apparently weak link with the ongoing talk. The relationship of what is said to the topic under discussion is not made clear.

7   The child often has difficulty in being explicit when he talks about experiences beyond the concrete present or his own personal needs and wants.

8   The child does not easily relate relevant past experiences to present experiences.

9   Even though the child may readily report on the present experiences and on past experiences, he does not spontaneously look for association and relationships. He does not give reasons and justifications and has difficulty in planning, in projecting into others' feelings and unfamiliar situations, and in imagining.

*Talk for Teaching and Learning* (pp 69-70)

This is a picture of the limited or under-achieving child, especially the kind that leads teachers to ask 'Yes, but how can we give them the language?' Joan Tough is no more than the most practical of all the specialists in this field who have realized that the question asks for an answer that does not fit the nature of language: it is not a linear set of objectives to fulfil. Joan Tough goes on, in some 150 pages of very straightforward exposition, to suggest a better answer. Such a child learns only through talk – but simple chat, or talk with friends, won't do: the teacher has to adopt new talk strategies, take part in talk with conscious awareness of what kinds of questions to use and what kinds to avoid. How to do this, and how to build on it, her book describes in detail, mainly through examples. One of the lessons to draw is that it is especially the non-talking child with whom it may be more useful to discuss a piece of writing before rather than after, and important to go round the room while the writing is taking place offering stimulus here, corrections there, and a quick re-planning job with the child who runs out of steam.

Most kinds of disadvantage and handicap are associated with some degree of slowness in language learning at some stage, but the frequency with which physically handicapped people achieve academic qualifications at Advanced Level or degree level should warn us of the danger of supposing that a retardation is always permanent. In any case, the inclusion of many kinds of special-need children in the ordinary school is a positive advantage: if the building can cope with a wheelchair, disabled pupils are a valuable part of the social experience of able-bodied ones. But the benefits may also be more narrowly educational. The group which is most readily incorporated tends to be the hearing-impaired, often with an adult ancillary and special communications equipment. The experience of ancillary workers in this situation is illuminating. They regularly have to simplify worksheets and blackboard tasks so that their vocabulary falls within the more limited scope of the hearing-impaired child's vocabulary – for example, 'Describe volcanic action, with the aid of diagrams' becomes 'Write about how volcanoes work, and draw pictures. . .'. Seeing this, other less able children in the set tend to attach themselves to the hearing-impaired in search of this kind of help and the guidance that goes with it. A sensible teacher will encourage that, while a wise one will modify her classroom style, and even her subject language, in search of improved grasp among the less able third of her class. This topic has very wide implications throughout secondary education, for teachers of all subjects. It was explored in a classic study by Douglas Barnes mentioned in the notes, but the pity is that so many teachers remain unaffected by it – until a hearing-impaired child joins the class.

In teaching a whole class where the educational centre of gravity is very low, once again the temptation to set exercises needs resisting: if the teacher needs time in which the pupils cannot have her full attention, it is better for each child to pursue individual reading books, in silence – and such a class should have some time doing that every day and even twice a day. The evidence of the Nottingham research on SRA Reading Laboratories was that they can provide valuable gains if they are used as short-term intensive devices, but as routine classroom fodder they lose much of that advantage. If exercises are set, it is as well to be discriminating about which ones. Chapter 2 suggests that course-book work that bases very obvious questions on very short passages is not worth while, but such course books may include exercises on other aspects of language that some children need – formation of plurals, for example, the different forms of given verbs, and exercises which show how words cluster together in families. The hesitation about exercises is not just prejudice. It rests on the same basis as the belief that proficiency in reading is the only index of progress that matters. This belief is accentuated by parental concern, but the leading specialist in this field, W. K. Brennan, has this to say:

> Language is most meaningful for slow learners when related to perceptual experience – to direct sensory input from something which the pupil is *doing*.

A concrete example arises in the curious coincidence which enabled me to see two classrooms on the same day: in one, the teacher believed in high standards of spelling and adopted thematic groupings of words for his weekly spelling test, which that day was about the words describing church buildings – transept, chancel, clerestory among them; in the other, a much less able class had been to a large church, and they were writing up in their topic folders the diagrams-with-labels they had brought back from the visit on their clip-boards. As with upper-secondary pupils, the question to ask first about children who fail is about the education they fail at.

## English as a second language

We have just seen one example of the contrast between the commonsense layman's view of slower learners, with its emphasis on 'being given language' and pressure on reading attainment, and the professional view that there may be more important things to attend to first. Just the same difference appears in the context of children who come into English-speaking classrooms with little or no English available. The commonsense view would be that they need to be packed off to a specialist centre for intensive language instruction. Well, this has been tried in several parts of the country, indeed in several countries, and it does not work. For whatever reason, children taught English in separate centres do not use it when they go back to mainstream schooling: if they are to learn an English they will use, they have to learn it where they will use it. The reason for this paradoxical finding lies in the social nature of language: who we are talking with matters quite as much as our formal command of vocabulary and structure, and children need to feel sure of their hearers as well as their wording.

This principle is at work in every well-run infant classroom: children who are learning to talk and to read are surrounded with stimuli, things to talk about, and whether these are visible objects in the room or daily experiences drawn out by the teacher, most of them will be given labels to convey the words and meanings – and the idea that potentially everthing in life can be signed in this way. Imagine the effect on ordinary infants of sending them to school and then taking them by bus to a Reading Centre to be taught how to read – yet when just this was done for immigrant children nobody thought it at all strange. The physical separation of the ESL learner needs to be as limited as possible, and withdrawal instruction needs to be for brief sessions in the same building. This is why most government funding for local work with ethnic minorities is channelled now into peripatetic and support teaching rather than special centres for pupils. The logic of this policy has consequences for ordinary teachers, which we can summarize under four main headings.

**1 Pupil needs** ESL learners are learning the language in all subjects, and learn best if the work in them recognizes their needs. Thus, new information and words are best grasped if there is visual or pictorial support. Every subject has its technical vocabulary to label in this way: square, triangle, circle, angle; map, river, coast, mountain, sea; year, date, reign, century, government; prayer, good, bad, right, wrong; poem, story, question, answer, interrupt –

the vast amount that native speakers take for granted about their language. ESL learners grasp these labelled objects and ideas best in the context, not of drills or word-lists, but of purposeful activities where they occur naturally. Almost all ESL learners, moreover, learn more successfully if they have free access to their mother-tongue in the face of difficulty: being able to talk briefly to a fellow-speaker of Gujerati or Greek is often useful, and being able to do so without feeling disapproval is very important. (The total-immersion principle of forbidding access to or use of the native language while learning another does serious harm if it is applied too early.)

**2 Teacher needs** the ability to monitor the learner's progress is not difficult to acquire, especially if it is informed by an understanding of how a child's native language can influence the learning. (For example, in Urdu and related languages verbs tend to come at the end of a sentence, and to combine the sentence-ending function of our full stop, with predictable effects on an Urdu-speaker's English. Other eastern languages lack our system of number or our system of tense, and so on.) More important, perhaps, is the need to understand how a school subject makes use of a range of distinctive language functions. Thus, science involves descriptions of process, sequence, possibility, predictions of outcome or success or failure, and a complex range of identifications of objects, connections and causes. History entails managing the expression of probability and of qualification, of degrees of importance as between causes and effects in major events. All these, and their equivalents in other subjects, have their distinctive wordings. A particular problem area among these wordings is that in which *square* or *force* occur in history, physics, mathematics and English. These considerations explain why some ESL attention may be necessary all the way through an 11–18 school. Teachers need also to understand that ESL learners whose native tongues are not usually found in written form may not understand our equation of writing with working, let alone the idea that writing may best be pursued through a process of drafting.

**3 Materials** we have referred already to the need to interweave words and objects, wordings and activities, and the same principle holds for the oral and the written. ESL learners naturally encounter a variety of accents in English, and only occasionally find this a problem, but opportunity for widening this experience is available through the media. Much more serious, though, is the unexamined nature of many school work-sheets and textbooks. The foreign learner is particularly at risk from the comprehension exercise that asks questions about the meanings of words without engaging either the pursuit of real-life meaning or any context outside the passage. The worksheet which has never been checked for its readability is another danger, and the methods suggested by Clive Sutton's book (mentioned in the notes) are very useful here.

**4 Attitudes** we have already noted that to deprive the ESL learners of access to the mother tongue can be a real impediment. However, if that access is to be freely available when it matters, there has to be a strongly counter-intuitive change of attitude in teachers and pupils. After all, two pupils conversing in a language the rest of the class do not understand are all too readily perceived as shutting the others out, and even if that feeling is not present, the two may avoid such discussion for fear of generating it. It is therefore important to have all teachers understand the point and make it very publicly understood by their pupils: the tolerance involved is not possible in a single classroom if the school climate is unsupportive. Much the same holds for the teacher's response to what she may see as incorrect usage, because ordinary adults and children see this rather differently from teachers. Sylvaine Wiles tells a story that puts it neatly:

Mother:     What did you do at school today?
Child (5):   I done apparatus and I done reading...
Mother:     Oh, you *did* apparatus and reading, *did* you?
Child:      ...and I done writing and I done painting...
Mother:     Did, darling, I did painting.
Child:      Mummy, if you don't listen to what I'm saying I won't tell you what I did at school today!

Few preconceptions are more misleading, or more offensive to the children involved, than the fixed belief that non-standard forms of expression reflect sub-standard forms of intellect.

## Accent and dialect

There is a story told, perhaps apocryphal. of a research worker who wanted to investigate some aspect of language and social class. He had asked some teachers to identify pupils at the extremes of the social spectrum, in order to expose the mismatch between the social background of the pupils identified in this way and the notions the teachers had about them. When the first couple of girls came in to see him, in a particularly 'nice' girls' grammar school, he explained the tasks he would ask them to carry out, with his tape-recorder at the ready. One of the girls asked, sweetly, whether they should use 'school talk' or 'home talk'. It transpired that the girls were equally fluent in the excessively 'correct' or 'nice' speech required by the school and the distinctly local Merseyside speech of their home community. The same held for all the other girls he interviewed, and what began as a study of some length lay completed in his hands in a couple of days.

This pattern is not new. The English school system has always had large numbers of pupils who could switch at will from one language variety to another. What does seem relatively new is the readiness of such young people to admit the fact. It seems that we have lived, over the past 30 years or so, through a transformation of social values about speech accent. Half a century ago the great majority of British people regarded their local or regional speech as having less prestige than the standard or non-regional form associated with 'BBC English'. Adults now in their 40s and 50s who have acquired non-regional speech are quite used to having parents 'who regard their own local or regional accents as something to be less than proud of. But their children now in their 20s find this sense of shame utterly incomprehensible: they retain their regional and local accents with pride both as university students and as manual labourers. So while the older generations may be uncomfortable with the accents of their grandchildren, taken all round there is much less hypocrisy and pretence about accent in England now than there was two generations ago.

This change in society's values does not quite remove the tedious nuisance of the parent who treat it as a school's 'duty' to teach its pupils to speak 'nice' or 'correct' English. A school should make no concessions to this particular snobbery. Children speak the language of their parents unless they want to do otherwise; if they seek the protective colouring of local speech at school, that should be accepted – the child will be able to make wider choices in time. The parent who objects that 'the school is teaching my child nasty words' needs to be gently disabused of the illusions involved. There is always a modest market for lessons in 'elocution', which are of little or no educational benefit, and should not be confused with the expertise of the speech therapist, whose aims do not include giving a child a prestige form of accent.

It is not only in the matter of prestige that accent differs from dialect. Technically a dialect is a variety of a language which has a vocabulary and grammatical forms that are its own. Most native speakers of a language can get the gist of most of its dialects, unless the users of a dialect set out to exclude others from understanding it, and most dialect speakers can also speak the standard language involved if they have to. However, the languages of some areas of the world are not dialects at all, notably the Creoles of the Caribbean. There is not space here to explain their origin, but they illustrate another general truth about language variety that bears repeating here: it is not disappearing. Our attitudes to language have drawn for many years on the belief that linguistic diversity would be bound to decline, chiefly under the influence of the media. Some dialect usages are disappearing, certainly, but that seems to reflect social and economic change much older and more enduring than newspapers and TV. The evidence from many parts of the world suggests that local variation is very far from dying out.

The journalistic theorizing that broadcasting would iron out all local accents is not very strongly supported by the available evidence. Provençal French is no closer in its resemblance to Parisian than it ever was. A reasonably good ear can tell a man from California apart from one from Oklahoma, and either from a Pennsylvanian. The Western Australian is as easily recognized in Sydney as he used to be. Within British English the same appears to hold good for its thousands of local variants, and we hear them spoken on the allegedly destructive radio, and spoken with pride, all the time. The quality of pride in local speech runs through much of the teaching profession as well as through its pupils and their families.

It would be naive, however, to suppose that the proud user of a local speech form is using it because he has no choice. The research worker whose subjects asked whether they should use 'home talk' or 'school talk' was encountering

117

the now quite normal phenomenon of accent switching, the ability to adopt the speech form appropriate to the situation.

Such a capacity to switch used to be regarded by many teachers as in some way a deception, an enjoyment of being two-faced or dishonest. The reality of life for most children is itself two-faced: it presents them with the familiar patterns of ordinary speech on one face, and the often slightly artificial patterns of school and the media on the other. That being so, learning to manage both with equal fluency and style is a valuable achievement. Unfortunately that fact runs headlong into conflict with one of the most deep-seated linguistic myths of our school system – that a child will learn to write standard English only if he first learns to speak it. The speech forms of very many university students and teachers today demonstrate conclusively that this is a fallacy. The need in the classroom between 9 and 14 is to master the patterns and requirements of written English, and the wider the linguistic distance between the pupils' speech patterns and the written language the more obvious the contrasts become – and the more easily segregated out for systematic instruction. Much of the response to this need has been set out in Chapter 7.

By the same token, the linguistic and social diversity of our society is useful classroom material if it is handled sensitively. There are many areas to explore – any aspect of social life and custom which is different will have its associated set of terms. Perhaps the most revealing are the forms of address. Most Asian languages employ a more complex and subtle social etiquette than English can express. They select pronouns of address not only according to the rank of the person addressed but also according to the relative difference in rank between that person and the speaker. One of the reasons for exploring the similarities and differences in the languages represented in the multi-ethnic classroom it its recognition of those languages. But an even stronger reason is that it may begin to undermine the linguistic chauvinism of the English. It can only be good for children who live in an area of England very conscious of its accent differences from an area only a few miles off to realize that similar local loyalties operate in Karachi or Athens and that the Englishman's implicit belief in the superior virtue of his own language is shared by the children in his own class – who place the same belief in Hindi, Arabic, Gujerati, Cypriot Greek or whatever.

The urge to standardize in a living language is doomed to failure. The persistent belief that a local accent will place its user in some kind of educational disadvantage, simply as speech, is entirely understandable but misplaced. The attempt to implement that belief in schools must fail because society no longer endorses the suppression of local speech as a proper aim for parents, media or schools. Indeed, it must go beyond failure by making teachers look ridiculous or driving children into dissembling. In any case the policy diverts energy and support from a much more important objective, the fostering of a proper appreciation for the speech we hear all about us.

# Notes and references

**Introduction**

The Bullock Report was published under the title *A Language for Life* (HMSO, 1974) and a short pamphlet by the English group of H. M. Inspectorate is *Bullock Revisited* (HMSO, 1981).

The integration of all junior or middle school English into topic work is now so uncommon that I have omitted it. The best source of English-focused thematic treatment is still A. Lynskey, *Children and Themes* (Oxford, 1974). A useful treatment on a broader basis is P. Prosser, *The World on your Doorstep* (McGraw Hill, 1982) but it is at its weakest in its treatment of literature.

**Chapter 1  Reading for understanding**

The substance of this chapter can be pursued more fully in papers in E. Lunzer & K. Gardner, *The Effective Use of Reading* (Heinemann Educational for the Schools Council, 1979). The source of the research and advice on reading referred to is V. Southgate, H. Arnold, & S. Johnson, *Extending Beginning Reading* (Heinemann Educational for the Schools Council, 1979).

The poem by Kevin Myhill appeared in *Riverline*, the magazine of Wisbech Grammar School, when the author was 13 years old.

For a list of useful sources of poetry for classroom use see the notes for Chapter 5.

**Chapter 2  Teaching skilful reading**

The main ideas in this chapter have been practised in some classrooms for nearly 20 years. Their most accessible presentations are in C. Walker *Reading Development & Extension* (Ward Lock, 1974) and in the study pack published by the Open University for its course E231 Reading Development, which has been one of the most potent influences for good in this field. There have been many books and anthologies of research papers on reading since the mid-1960s. The most generally useful and balanced is probably J. Reid (Ed) *Reading: Problems and Practices* (Ward Lock, 1972).

The wider language context in which reading development occurs is the theme of another particularly valuable collection: N. Mercer, (Ed) *Language in School and Community* (Edward Arnold, 1981) which includes the paper by Katharine Perera on 'Some Language Problems in School Learning'.

**Chapter 3  The reading curriculum**

C. Harrison, *Readability in the Classroom* (Cambridge, 1980) has become the standard work, succeeding the pioneer book by Gilliland.

The books mentioned on children's literature are S. Egoff, G. T. Stubbs & L. F. Ashley, *Only Connect* (Oxford Canada, 1969); M. Meek, A. Warlow, G. Barton, *The Cool Web: The Pattern of Children's Reading* (Bodley Head, 1977);

F. Inglis, *The Promise of Happiness* (Cambridge, 1981); Course Pack P350, *Children, Language & Literature* (Open U.P., 1982).

Also to be welcomed in this field is D. Jackson, *Encounters with Books* (Methuen, 1983). The important essay by D. W. Harding, 'Psychological Processes in the Reading of Fiction' is reprinted in *The Cool Web* (pp 58–72).

The novel about the frightened boy in Victorian London is Leon Garfield's *John Diamond* (Kestrel/Puffin).

## Chapter 4  Development in writing

The London research is reported fully in J. Britton et al, *The Development of Writing Abilities (11–18)* (Macmillan for the Schools Council, 1975). A very readable investigation of writing in the junior age range, and one with many useful insights, is W. Harpin *The Second R* (Unwin, 1976) while the main published account of the Crediton inquiry is A. Wilkinson et al, *Assessing Language Development* (Oxford, 1980).

I am grateful, for permission, both to quote material and to make free use of his ideas, to G. Kress, *Learning to Write* (Routledge, 1982).

Other recent books on writing have contributed to my thinking: Donald Graves' *Writing: Teachers and Children at Work* (Heinemann, 1982) is full of human warmth but could have conveyed its points with greater clarity in half the length. Frank Smith's *Writing and the Writer* (Heinemann, 1982) is weightier and has some fascinating notes on the writing process as he experienced it.

The source of the treatment in Figure 3 is M. A. K. Halliday and R. Hasan, *Cohesion in English* (Longman, 1976) and Michael Halliday's other seminal papers in this field are in S. Rogers (Ed) *Children and Language* (Oxford, 1975).

Emlyn Williams' autobiography is entitled *George*.

## Chapter 5  Teaching writing

The need for material that would stimulate discussion and imagination led Barry Maybury to follow his book *Creative Writing for Juniors* (Batsford, 2nd Ed, 1981) with a set of six anthologies of prose, verse, short stories, pictures and drawings. They are among the best of their kind, and the relevant volumes are *Wordscapes, Thoughtshapes, Wordspinners, Thoughtweavers* (Oxford, 1970/ 1972/1981). The first two listed are intended for 9–11, the others for 11–13.

For the Junior age range are the *Storyhouse* books, which come in five levels but with much variation within each, with a valuable teacher's book and accompanying tapes, edited with verve and skill by David Jackson and Dennis Pepper (Oxford 1976/1979). The material is well adapted to group organization, provided the teacher reads the whole volume first.

A rather different source, which comes closer to realizing the full potential of language and offers what one might call a programme of inventive writing, is F. Skitt, *Themes for Language Learning* (Black, 1978). This material is practical, developed in sustained trial use, pertinent to any point in the 9–14 age range, and among the best new teaching material for some years.

The *Children as Writers* competition began under sponsorship of a national newspaper, but has changed publishers more than once. Your local librarian should be able to trace the annual publication of best entries.

The poem by Theodore Roethke quoted on page 60 is printed in several good poetry anthologies. His fine poem *The Meadow Mouse* is in Vol. 1 of R. Deadman & A. Razzell, *Awareness 1 & 2* (Macmillan, 1977). From the same publisher come a series edited by Frank Plimmer called *Inside Outside*, and my own source of *Child on Top of a Greenhouse*, a moving and sensitive collection called *As Large as Alone*, edited by Christopher Copeman and James Gibson.

## Chapter 6   Teaching the catching of spelling

The book by Christopher Jarman is *The Development of Handwriting Skills* (Blackwell, 1979). The Nelson handwriting scheme is now published as *New Nelson Handwriting* (1984) by Peter Smith et al.

The title of this chapter is an allusion to a work of genuine insight into the problems that English orthography poses for slower learners, M. Peters, *Spelling: Caught or Taught?* (Routledge, 1967). There is a remarkable degree of consonance between Margaret Peters' and my views of the spelling system in spite of some difference of view on what the nature of the system signifies for teaching. My position derives from K. A. Albrow, *The English Writing System* (Longman, 1972) and the largely (and regrettably) unpublished work of John Mountford (Southampton), much of which is fairly technical. Dr Albrow has pointed out that it is no part of the purpose of a writing system to tell us how a language should be pronounced, but the preoccupations of those who work with slow-learning children understandably lead them (and many teachers) to treat it as if it were. The first full-scale scholarly treatment, a difficult collection of research papers, is U. Frith (Ed) *Cognitive Processes in Spelling* (Academic Press, 1980) which among other things shows how intellectually flimsy is the case for spelling reform.

I am grateful for permission to reprint this chapter from *Education 3–13*.

## Chapter 7   Writing good modern English

'Write in good modern English' is the standard rubric of many GCE examination papers.

The standard authority for English punctuation is Appendix III of R. Quirk et al, *Grammar of Contemporary English* (Longman, 1972). This book is one of the great scholarly achievements of our time, superlatively laid out and printed, packed with fascinating material about the language. It also comes in a condensed version: R. Quirk et al, *A University Grammar of English* (Longman, 1973) but a more accessible treatment in modest paperback format is F. S. Scott et al, *English Grammar: A Linguistic Study* (Heinemann 1968). The approach to sentence structure that informs these three books, and which I prefer, also lies behind the series by Michael Newby, *Making Language* (Oxford, 1981).

My treatment of punctuation and sentencing seeks to take some account of the role of intonation in speech, which is well described in Chapter 5 of G. Brown, *Listening to Spoken English* (Longman, 1977).

The substance of part of this chapter first appeared in *The Use of English*.

## Chapter 8   Oral English

There is a quotation in Chapter 10 from the work of Joan Tough, and the book referred to there will provide many useful expansions of this chapter. It has absorbed what is useful from the thinking that was dominated by Bernstein's hypotheses, but dismisses the sentimental claptrap that ill-understood Bernsteinian ideas often generated in teachers who had never read him for themselves. Joan Tough's stance on unorganized and undirected classroom chatter is if anything more severe than my own.

Take Part Books are edited by Sheila Lane and Marion Kemp for Ward Lock. The Reports of the APU Language Unit are published by HMSO, and the first report on the Oracy programme can be expected late in 1984.

## Chapter 9  Putting it into practice

There are some useful ideas and guidance on group organization and how to move towards it in M. Bassey, *Practical Classroom Organisation in the Primary School* (Ward Lock, 1978).

The standard guide on classroom management for whole-class teaching is M. Marland, *The Craft of the Classroom* (Heinemann, 1975).

The Department of Education and Science issued late in 1983 a dossier of samples of writing done by 15 year olds, intended to give a range of material to show how well or badly such pupils write. The dossier gives no indication of the length of time allowed for the test pieces shown, or whether the selection published is typical in respect of scale and structure as well as in marks gained. The evidence certainly supports the finding that many pupils at 15 are writing less well than many others can do at 11, and would seem to support the view that existing criteria in CSE English are unacceptably lax. Whether a larger sample would give a similar impression remains to be seen, but the provisional conclusion for teachers of pupils up to 14 has to be that the critical years come before that age rather than after it.

On progression and assessment there is much helpful material in Schools Council Working Paper 75, *Primary Practice* (Methuen, 1983).

Harold Evans' *Pictures on a Page* is published by Heinemann (1978).

## Chapter 10  Some problem areas

**Drama**  There is a large literature, most of it seeking converts or written for prospective specialists. Longer than necessary but helpful is T. Stabler, *Drama in Primary Schools* (Macmillan, 1978) the report of a short Schools Council project. The most valuable book for non-specialists to learn from is J. Seely, *In Context* (Oxford, 1976) especially when filled out with the same author's loose-leaf stores of lesson material, *Dramakit* and *Playkits* (Oxford 1977/1980).

**Microcomputing**  This field changes with alarming rapidity, but good software which makes children think and discuss rather than perform mere robotic exercises remains in short supply. Most of the alleged benefits of the microcomputer for English in the middle years are specious. My own treatment of punctuation as integrally related to the meanings being represented will show why the rigidly rule-restricted programs designed to 'teach' punctuation are likely to convince pupils that writing is not for them. Fortunately there is a good, recent and humane book on the subject: Daniel Chandler's *Young Learners and the Microcomputer* (Open University Press, 1984).

**Special needs**   I am indebted to the help of my colleague Gordon Foster in assembling and assessing material for this section. The best general book may well be W. K. Brennan, *Curricular Needs of Slow Learners* (Evans/Methuen) while the same author's companion volume, *Reading for Slow Learners: a Curriculum Guide* (Evans/Methuen, 1982) takes the topic well into our age range. Joan Tough's *Talk for Teaching and Learning* is one of her most practical books, published by Ward Lock/Drake Educational. The literature about reading is immense and much so-called research in it is of little value. A book that stands out from the mass for its clarity and its respect for the magnitude of the task involved is M. Clay, *Reading: the Patterning of Complex Behaviour* (Heinemann, 1972). The paper by Douglas Barnes referred to in the text is in D. Barnes, (Ed) *Language, the Learner and the School* (Penguin, 1972), one of the most influential short books of its kind.

**English as a second language**   My colleague Henderson Clarke has contributed much of what I know in this field – sufficient to make me wary of suggesting that any teacher try to implement the suggestions given in this chapter without seeking specialist help, which should ideally not be remedial help. The aspects of this stance about language-learning that bear on pupils of all kinds, including native speakers of English, are usefully set out in C. Sutton, *Communicating in the Classroom* (Hodder, 1981).

The anecdote told by Sylvaine Wiles appears in her contribution to the collection edited by Neil Mercer which is mentioned in the Notes to Chapter 2. The multi-cultural perspectives that bear on all schools, not just the ethnically mixed ones, are well put in the excellent R. Willey, *Teaching in Multi-Cultural Britain* (Longman, 1983).

**Accent and dialect**   A basic account of the relevant definitions can be found in Chapter 10 of P. Doughty et al, *Exploring Language* (Edward Arnold, 1972). There is a good paper on speech variety by Mercer and Janet Maybin in Mercer's *Language in School and Community*, mentioned above. Relevant to this topic and to most sections of this chapter is Gahagan & Gahagan, *Talk Reform* (Routledge, 1975). A full discussion of the evidence for the view of accent and dialect taken here is Peter Trudgill's *Accent, Dialect and the School* (Edward Arnold 1975).

## List of novels mentioned

Paperback editions are listed where they are available.

Richard Adams   *Watership Down*   Kestrel/Puffin
Nina Bawden   *Carrie's War*   Puffin
Frances Hodgson Burnett   *The Secret Garden*   Puffin
Betsy Byars   *The Eighteenth Emergency*   Puffin
Betsy Byars   *The Midnight Fox*   Puffin
Eric Carle   *The Very Hungry Caterpillar*   Hamish Hamilton
Vera & Bill Cleaver   *Where the Lilies Bloom*   Puffin (OP)
Catherine Cookson   *The Nipper*   Puffin
Farrukh Dhondy   *East End at Your Feet*   Macmillan Topliner
Nicholas Fisk   *Snatched*   Hodder

Paula Fox   *The Slave Dancer*   Macmillan
Paula Fox   *How Many Miles to Babylon?*   Macmillan
Alan Garner   *The Owl Service*   Collins/Fontana
Alan Garner   *The Stone Book*   Collins
Eve Garnett   *The Family from One End Street*   Heinemann New Windmill
Leon Garfield   *John Diamond*   Kestrel/Puffin
John Gordon   *The House on the Brink*   Puffin Plus
Rosa Guy   *The Friends*   Puffin
Janet Hitchman   *The King of the Barbareens*   Puffin
Ann Holm   *I am David*   Puffin
Ted Hughes   *The Iron Man*   Faber & Faber
Gene Kemp   *The Turbulent Term of Tyke Tiler*   Puffin
Clive King   *Stig of the Dump*   Kestrel/Puffin
Ursula Le Guin   *The Wizard of Earthsea*   Puffin
C. S. Lewis   *The Lion, the Witch and the Wardrobe*   Puffin
Ruth Lingard   *Across the Barricades*   Puffin Plus
Penelope Lively   *The Ghost of Thomas Kempe*   Piccolo
Michelle Magorian   *Goodnight Mister Tom*   Kestrel/Puffin
Jan Mark   *Thunder and Lightnings*   Kestrel/Puffin
Jan Needle   *My Mate Shofiq*   Fontana Lions
Robert C. O'Brien   *Mrs Frisby and the Rats of NIMH*   Puffin
Phillippa Pearce   *Tom's Midnight Garden*   Puffin
K. M. Peyton   *Prove Yourself a Hero*   Oxford
David Rees   *The Exeter Blitz*   Heinemann New Windmill
Susan Sallis   *Sweet Frannie*   Heinemann
Ian Serraillier   *The Silver Sword*   Puffin
Esther Hautzig   *The Endless Steppe*   Puffin Plus
Rosemary Sutcliff   *The Lantern Bearers*   Oxford/Puffin
J. R. R. Tolkien   *Lord of the Rings*   Allen & Unwin
John Rowe Townsend   *A Foreign Affair*   Kestrel
Ruth Underhill   *Beaverbird*   ★OP
Jill Paton Walsh   *Fireweed*   Macmillan
Jill Paton Walsh   *The Dolphin Crossing*   Puffin Plus
Richard Westall   *The Machinegunners*   Puffin
E. B. White   *Charlotte's Web*   Puffin
John Wyndham   *The Midwich Cuckoos*   Longman Knockouts

★A play-format version exists in *Take Part Books*, ed. Lane & Kemp, (Ward Lock).

# Index